Pedro Dsouza

COLOR TEST

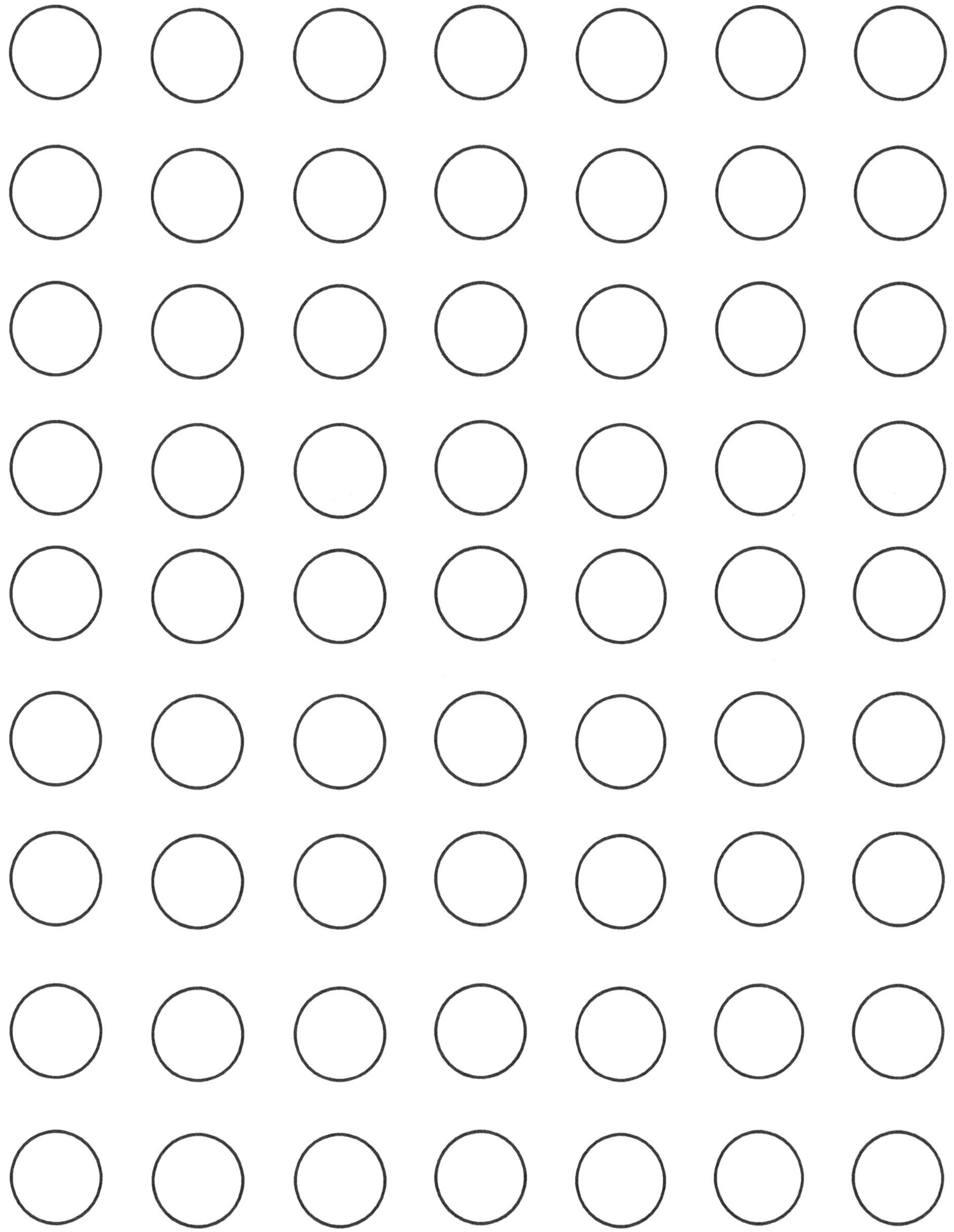

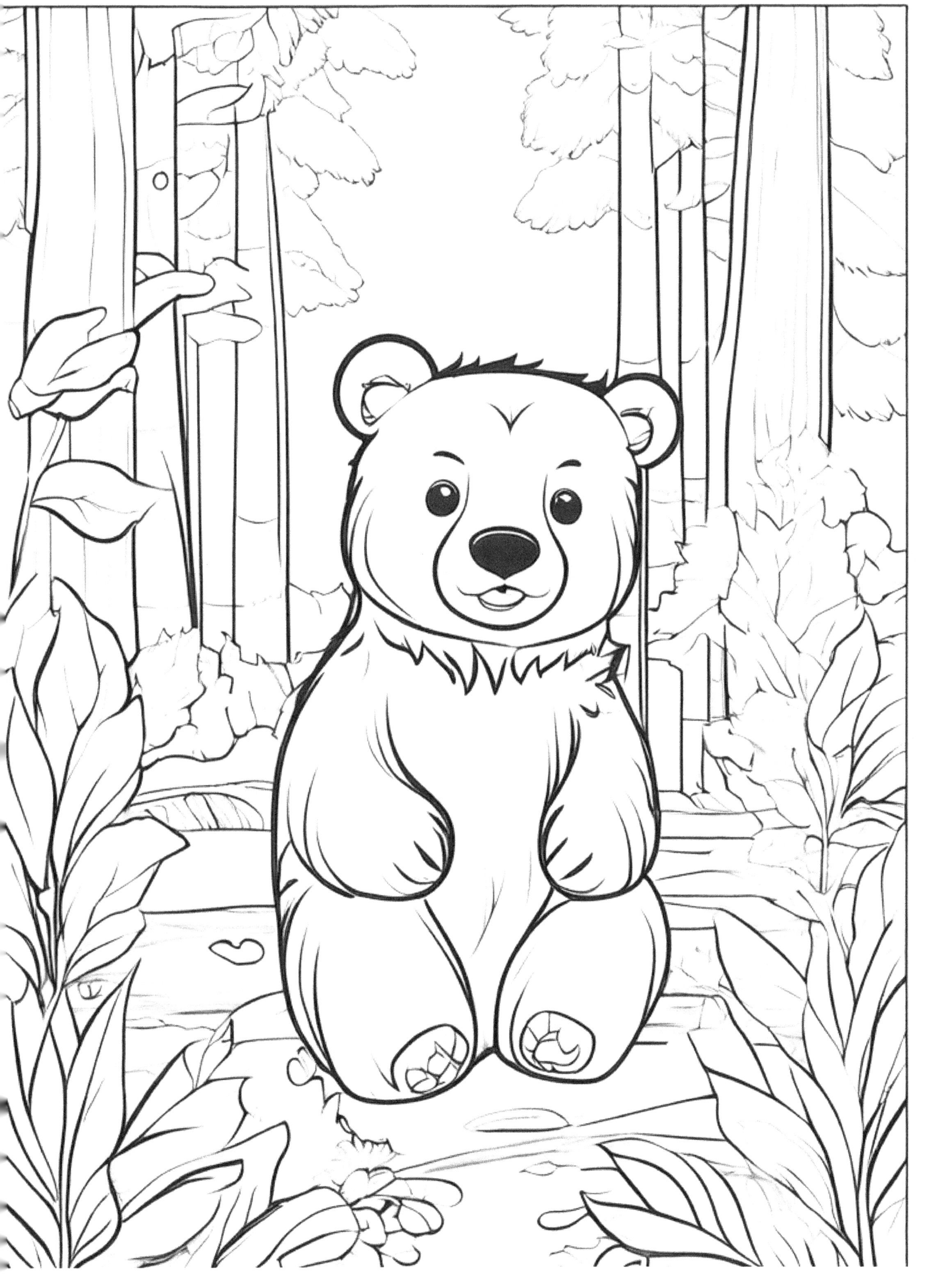

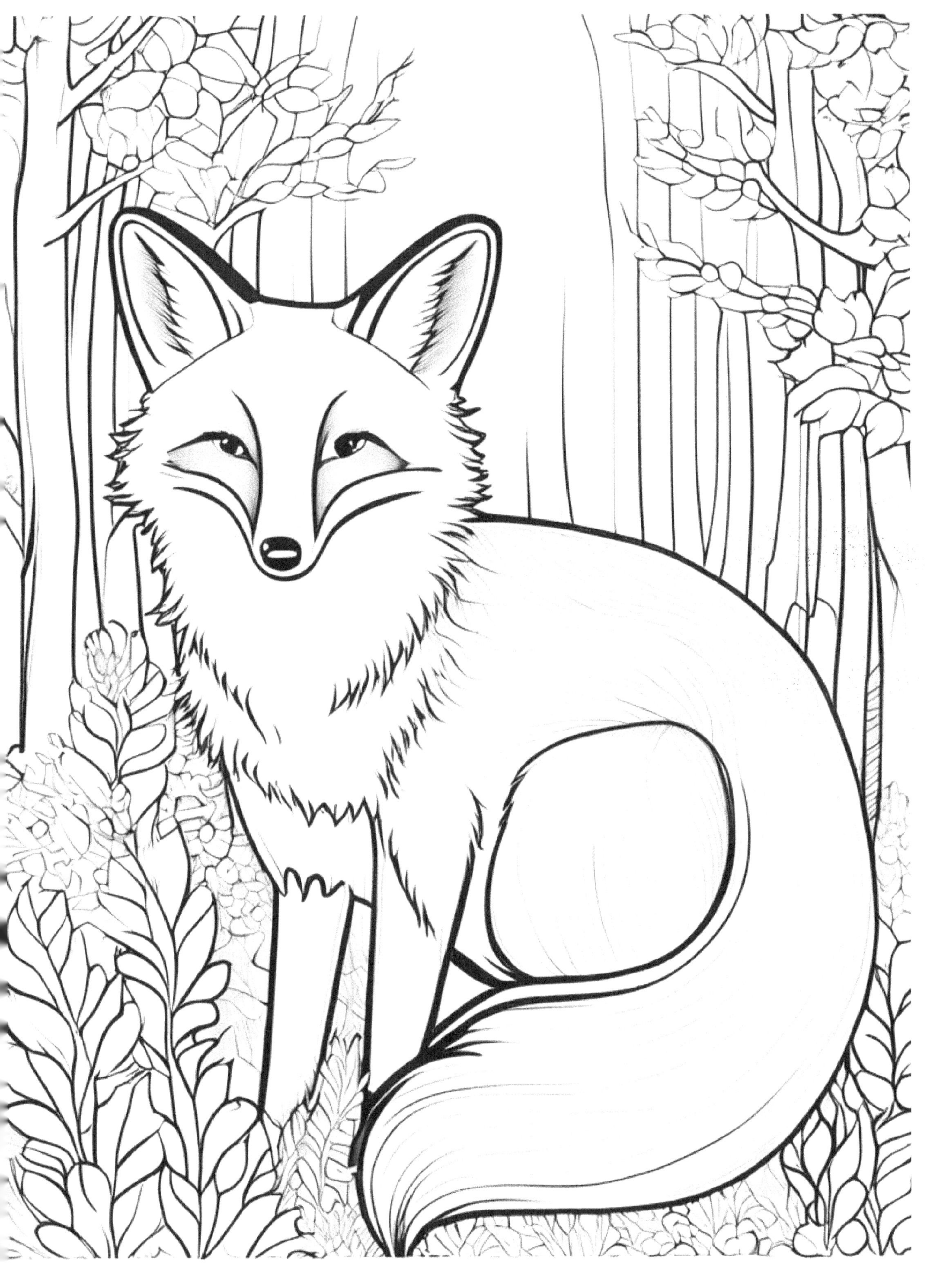

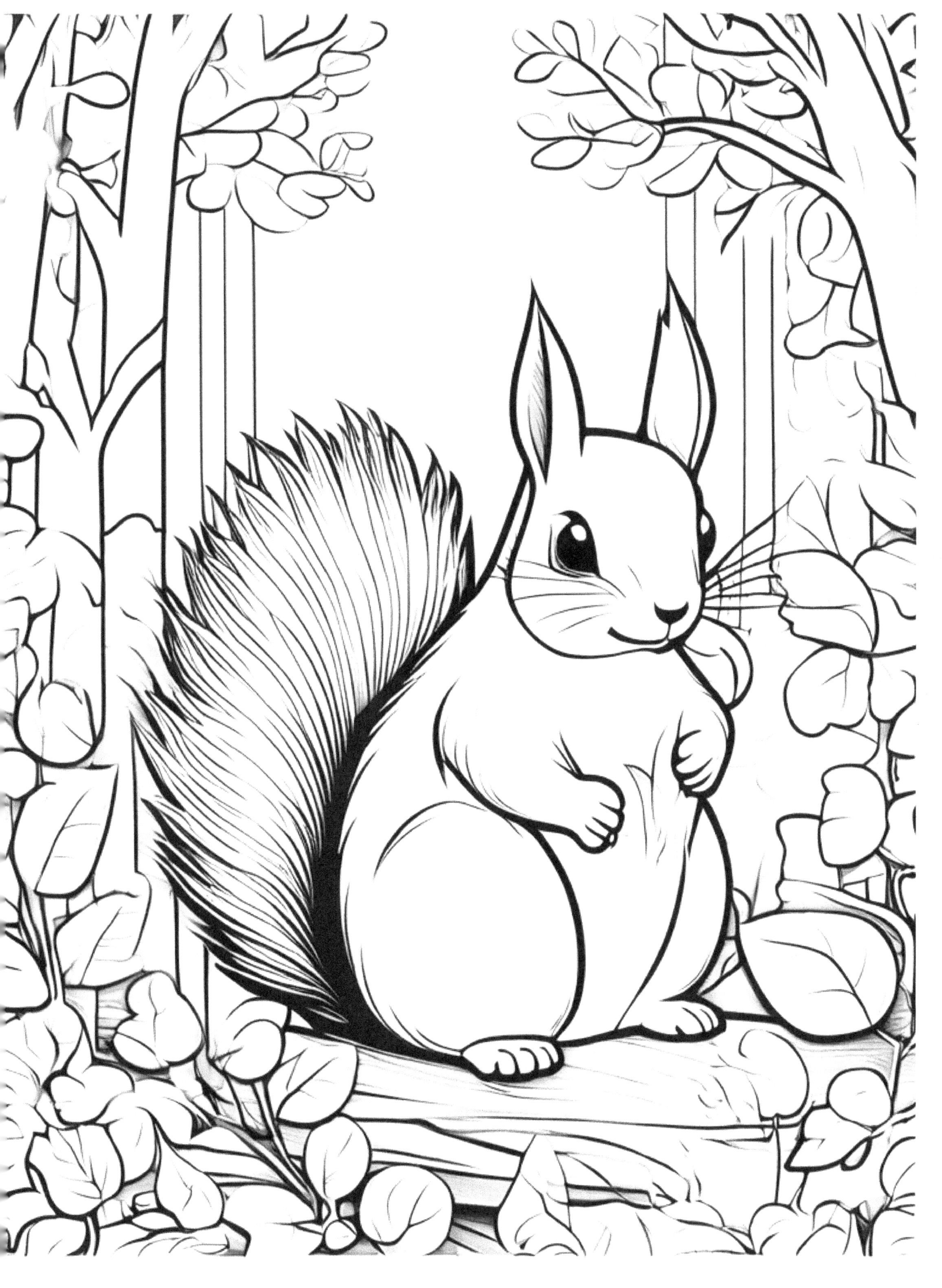

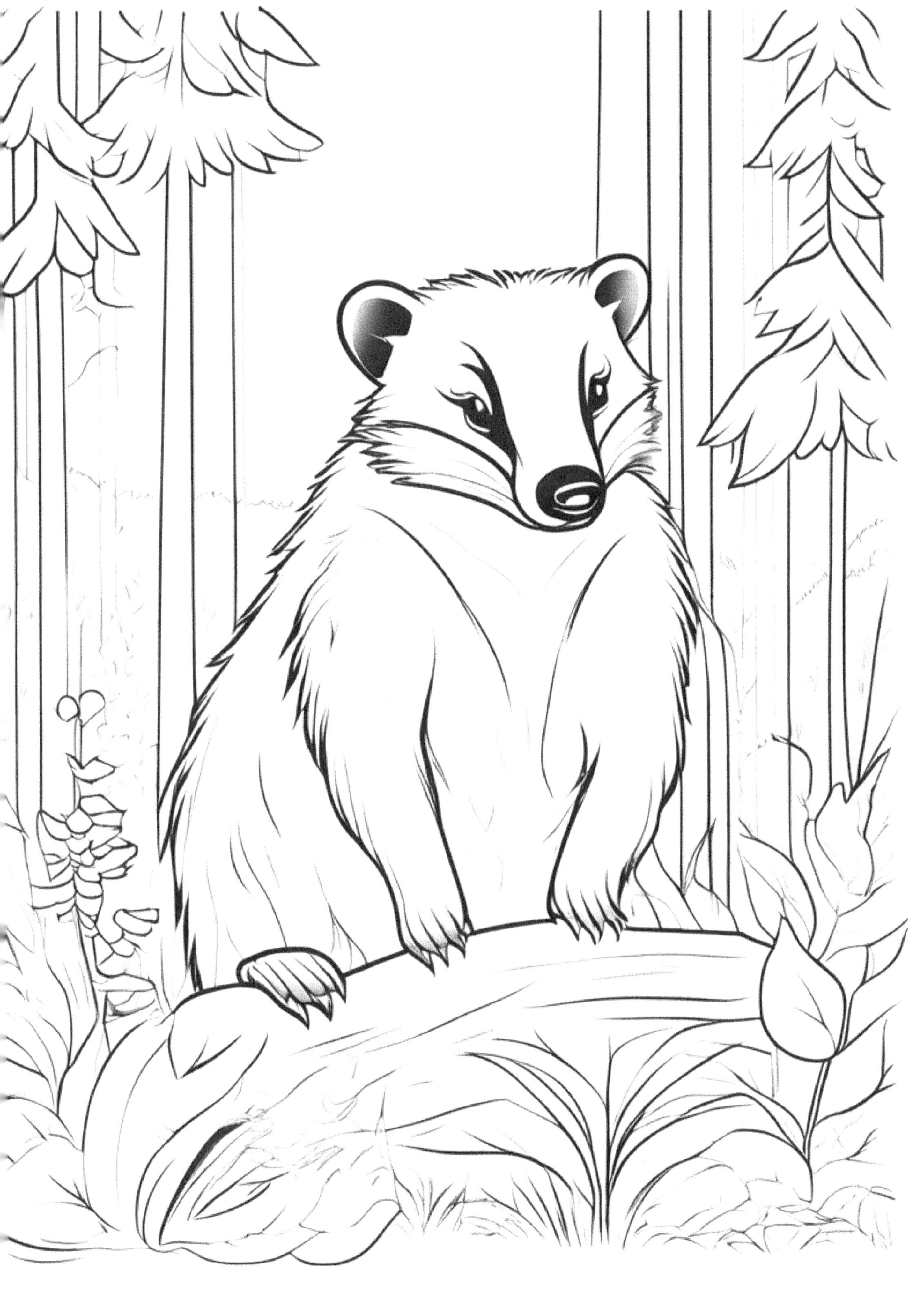

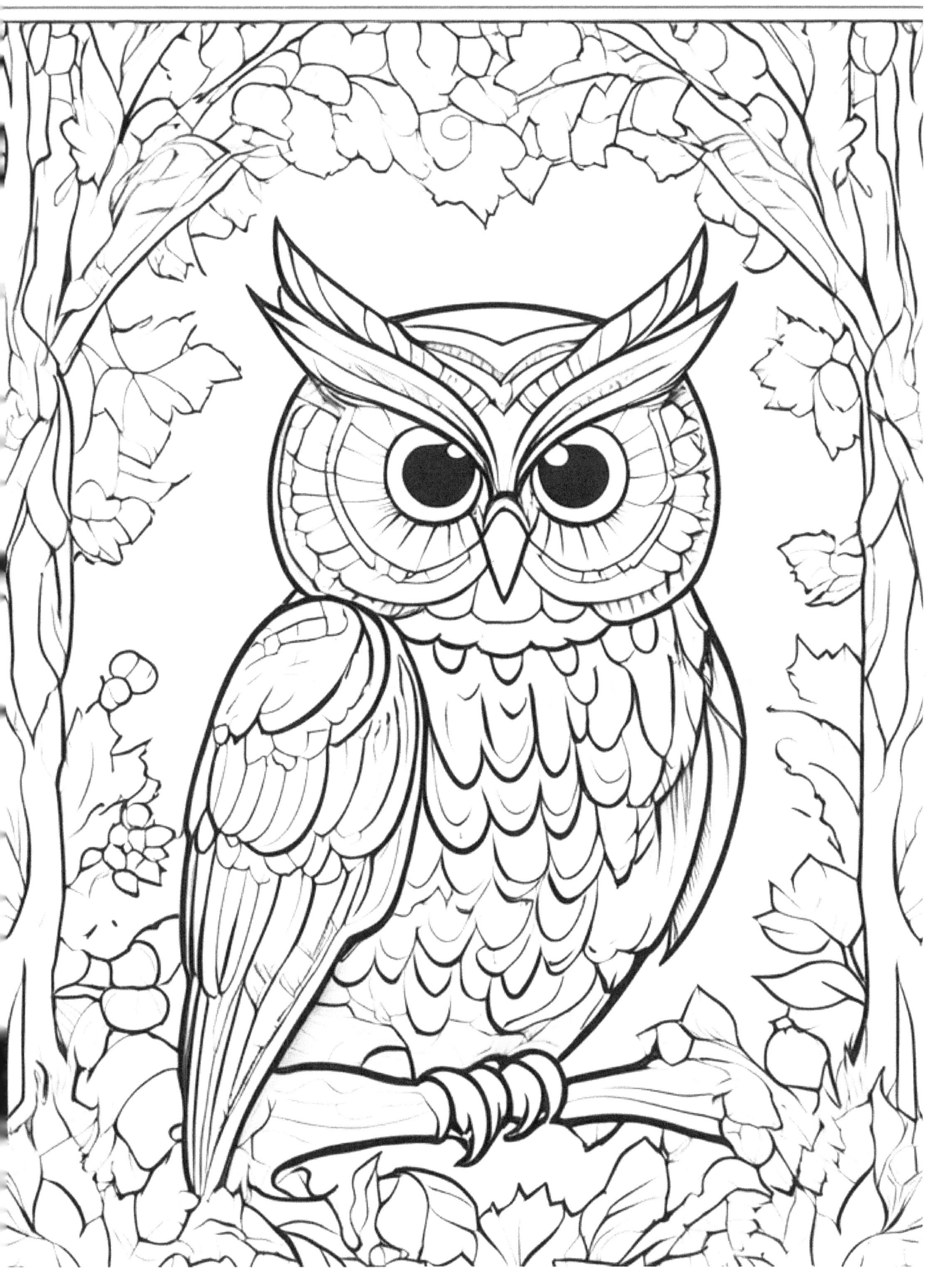

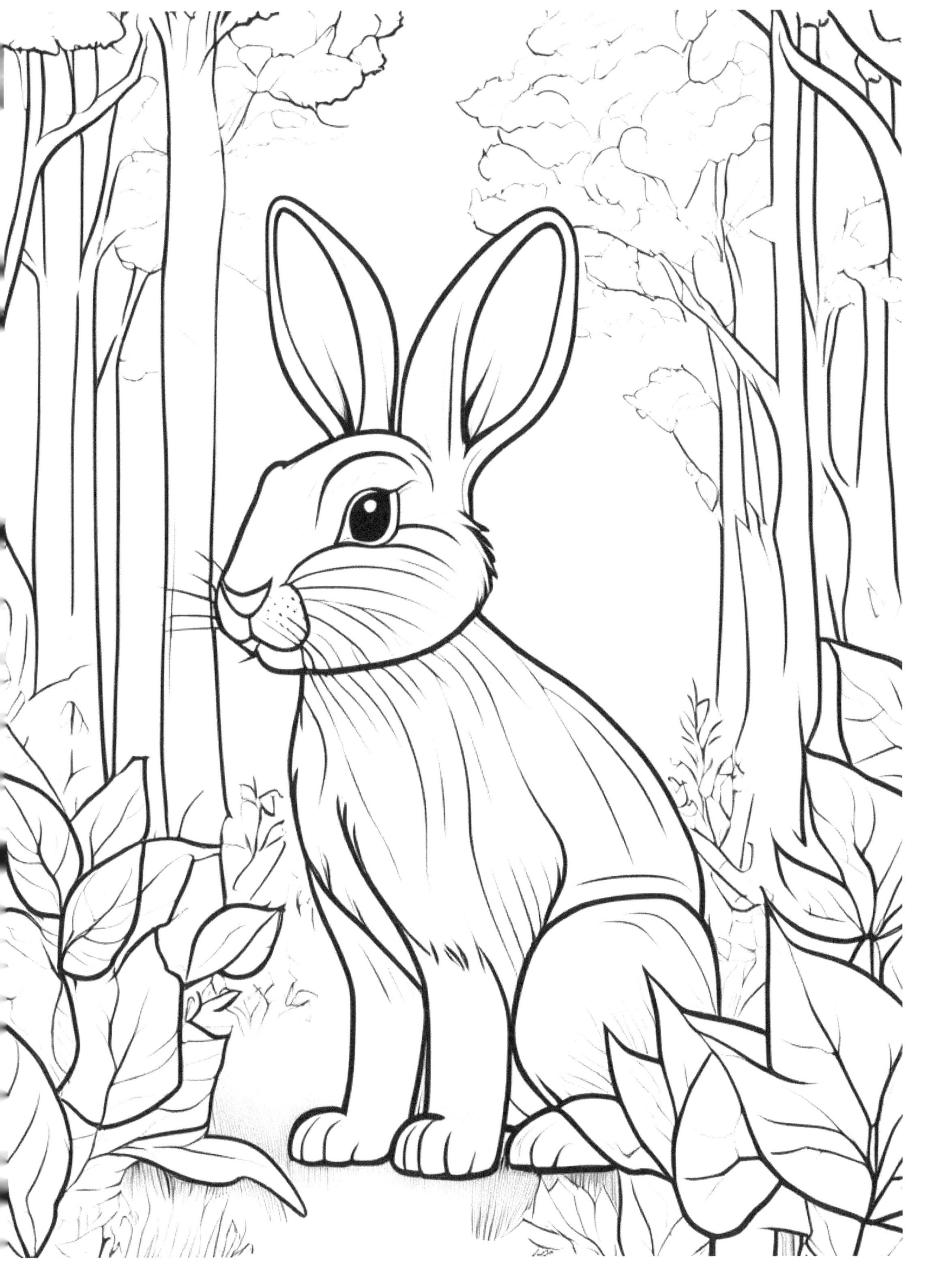

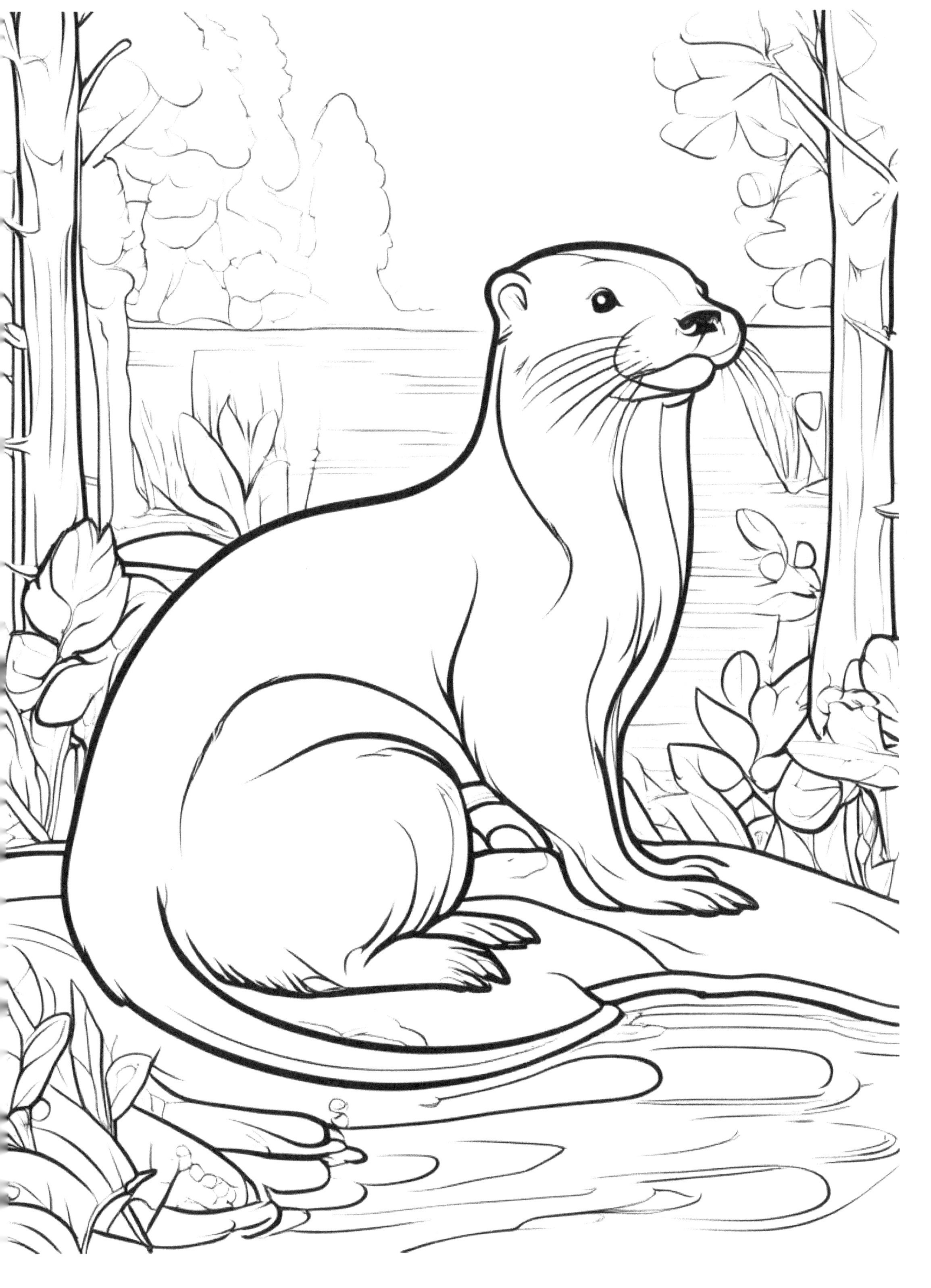

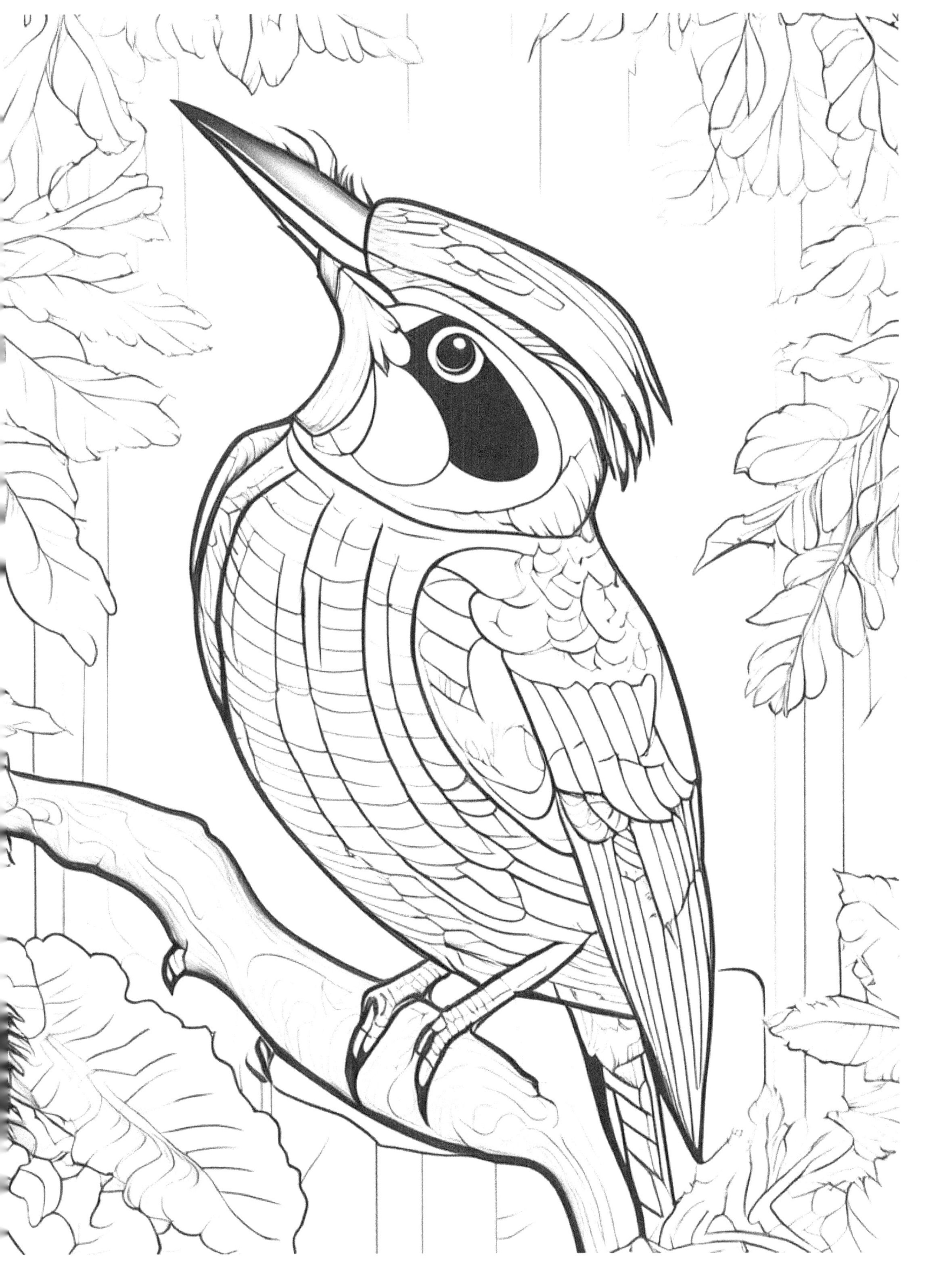

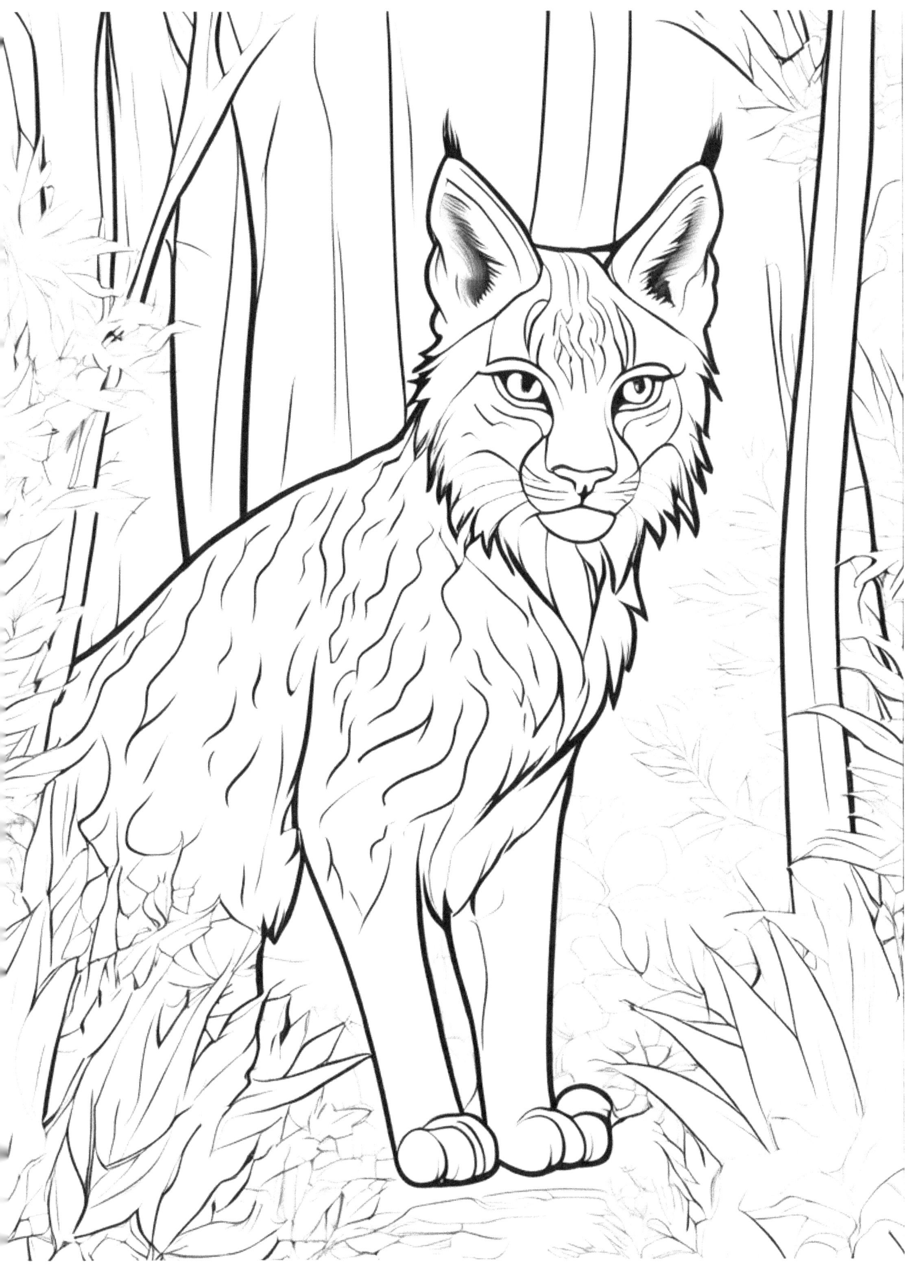

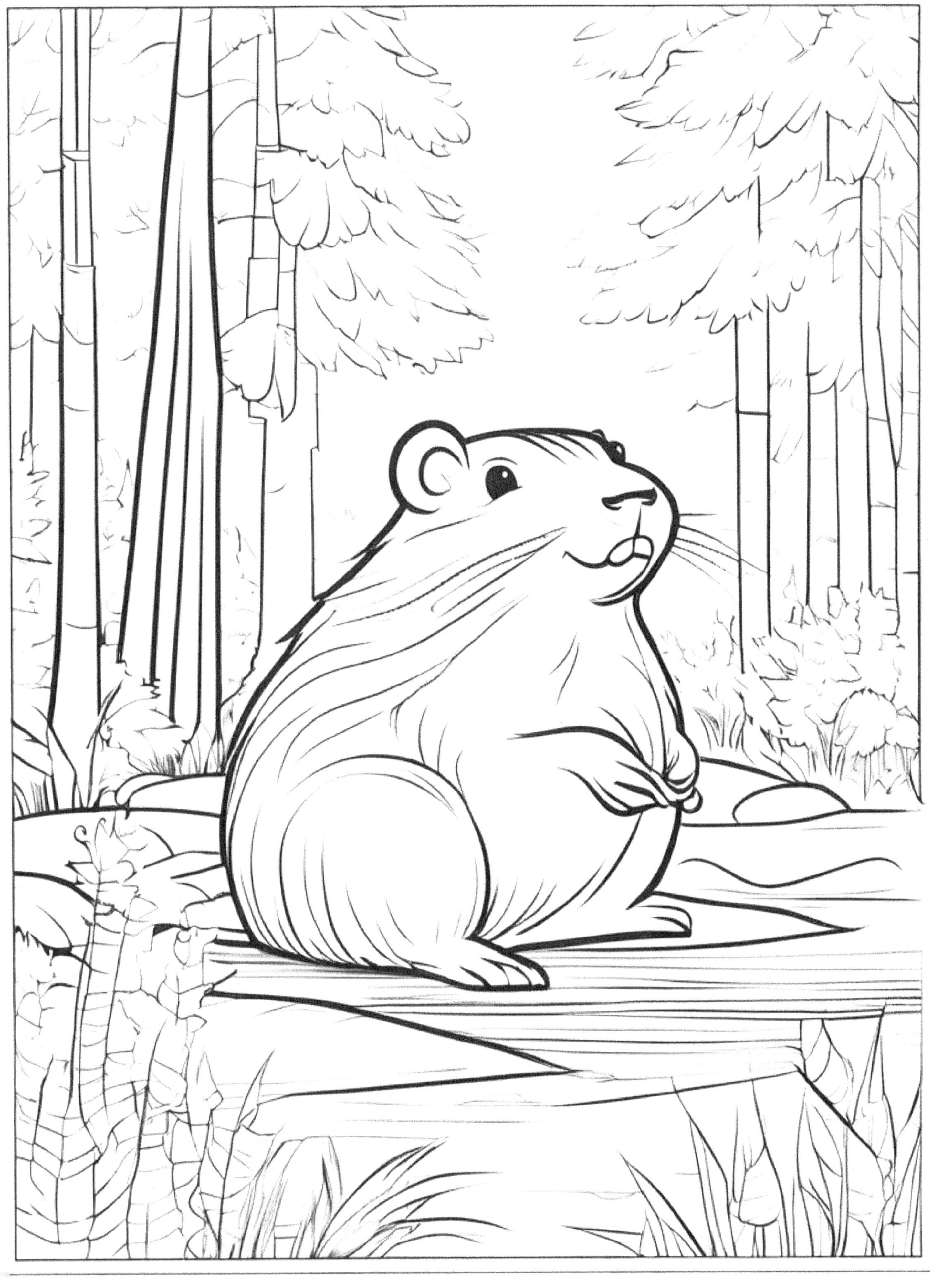

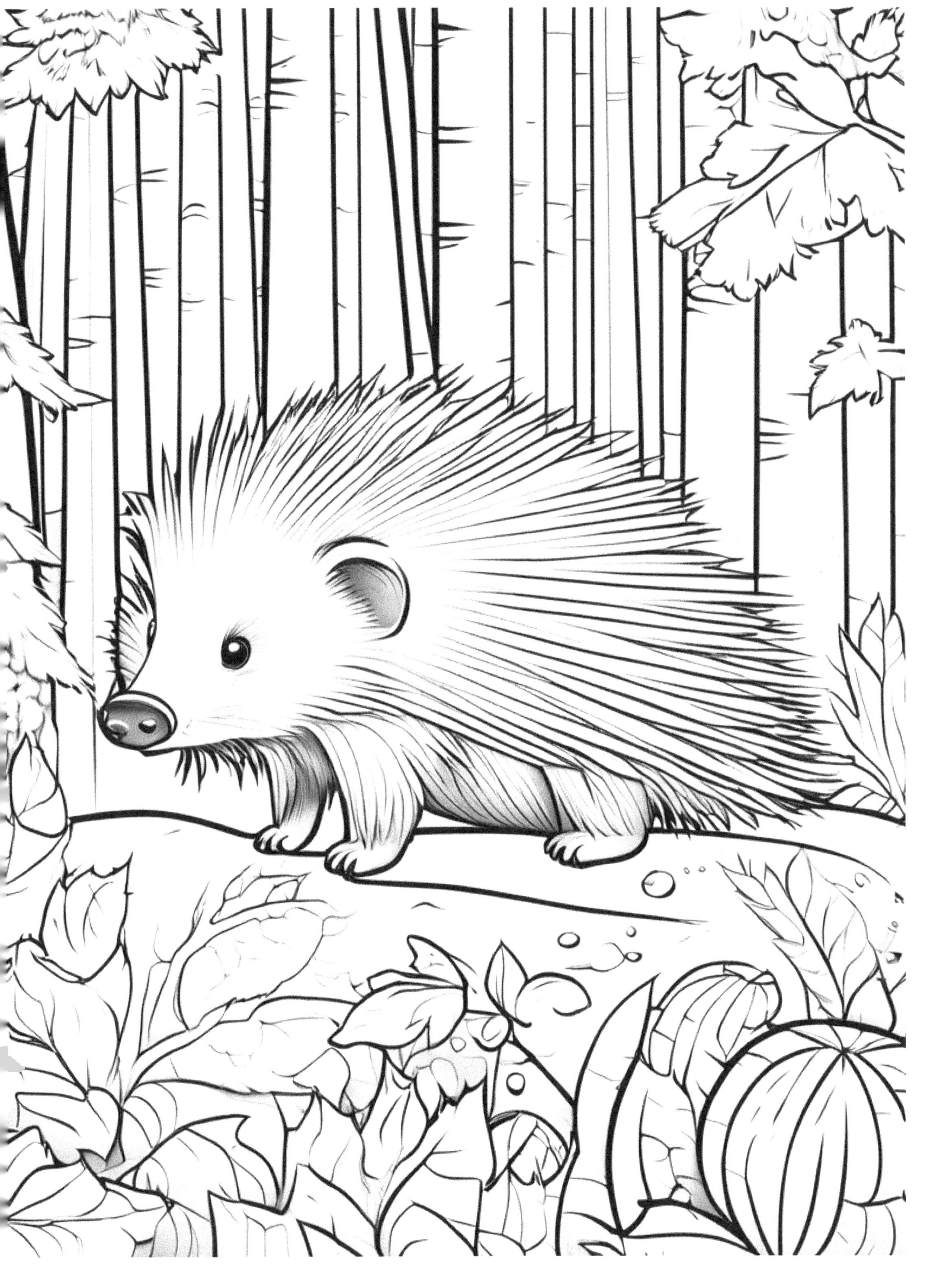

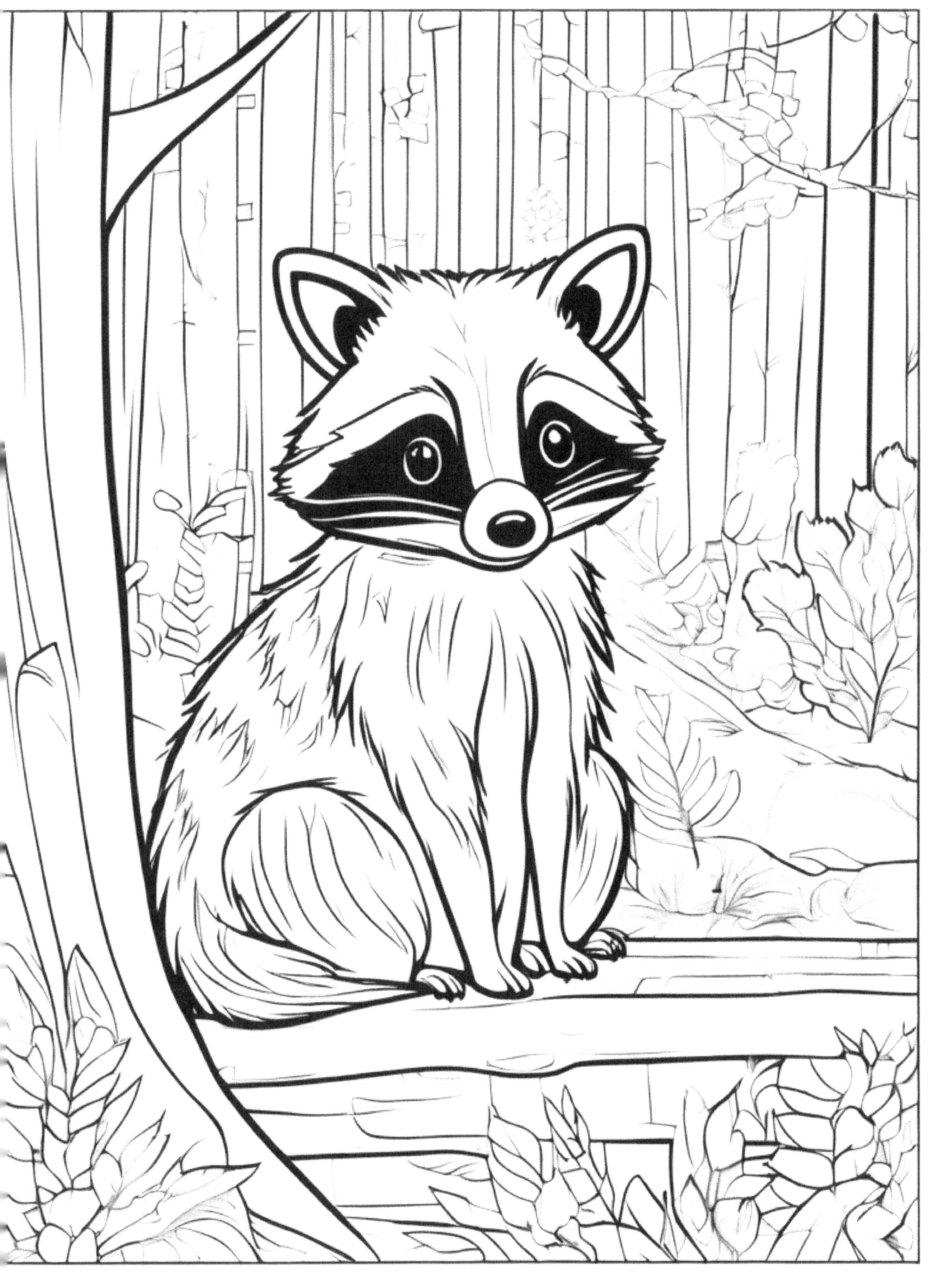

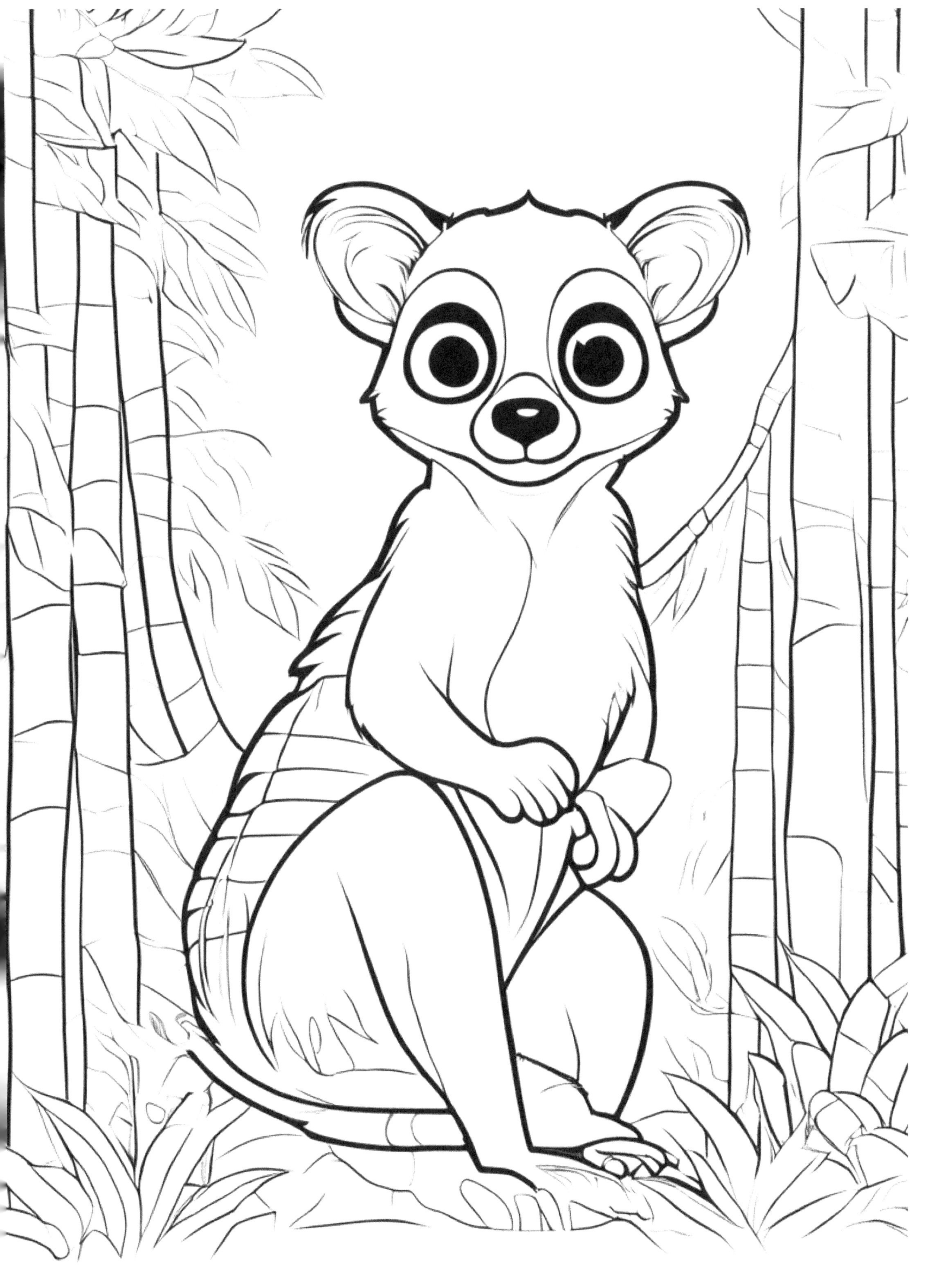

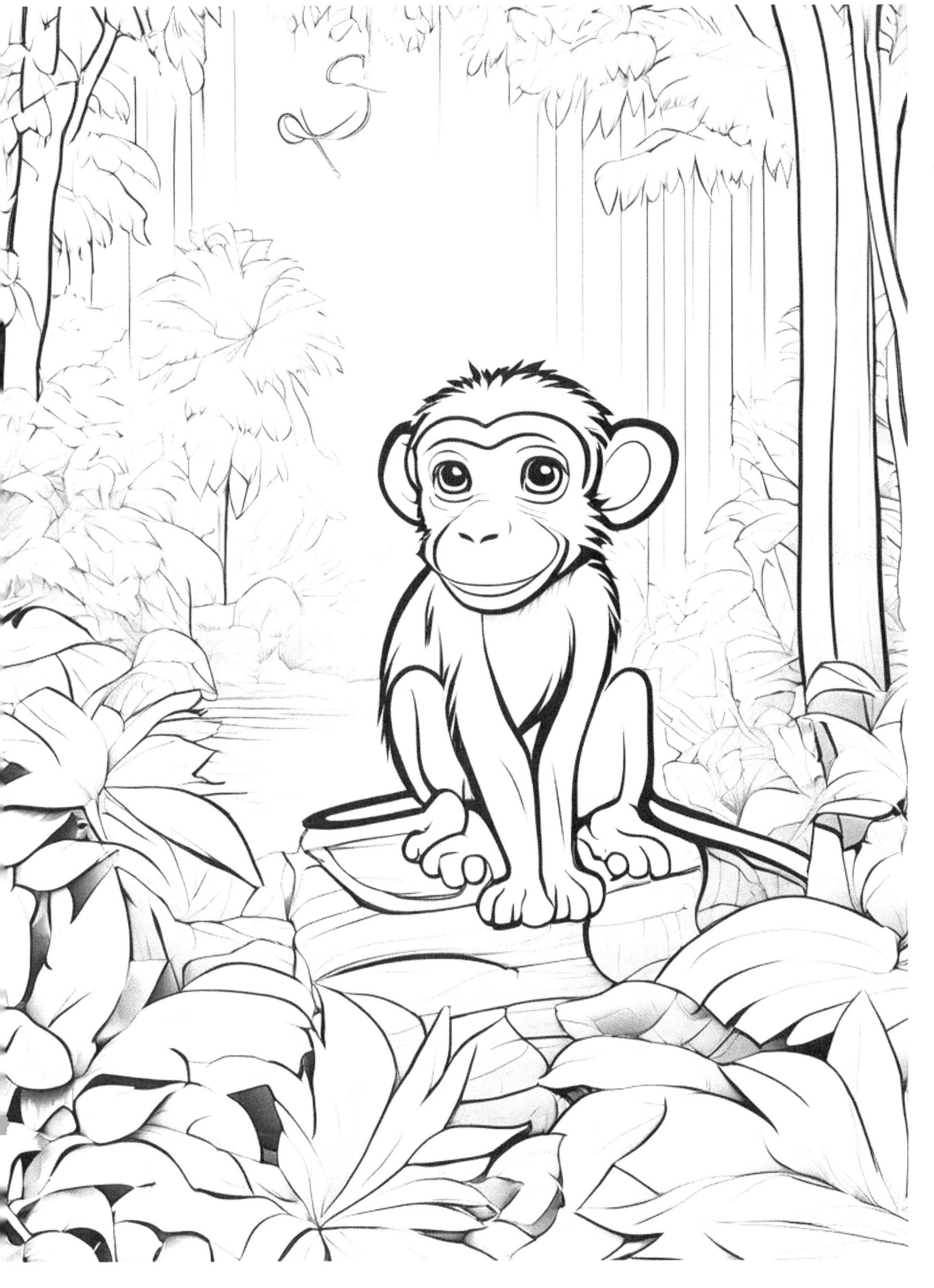

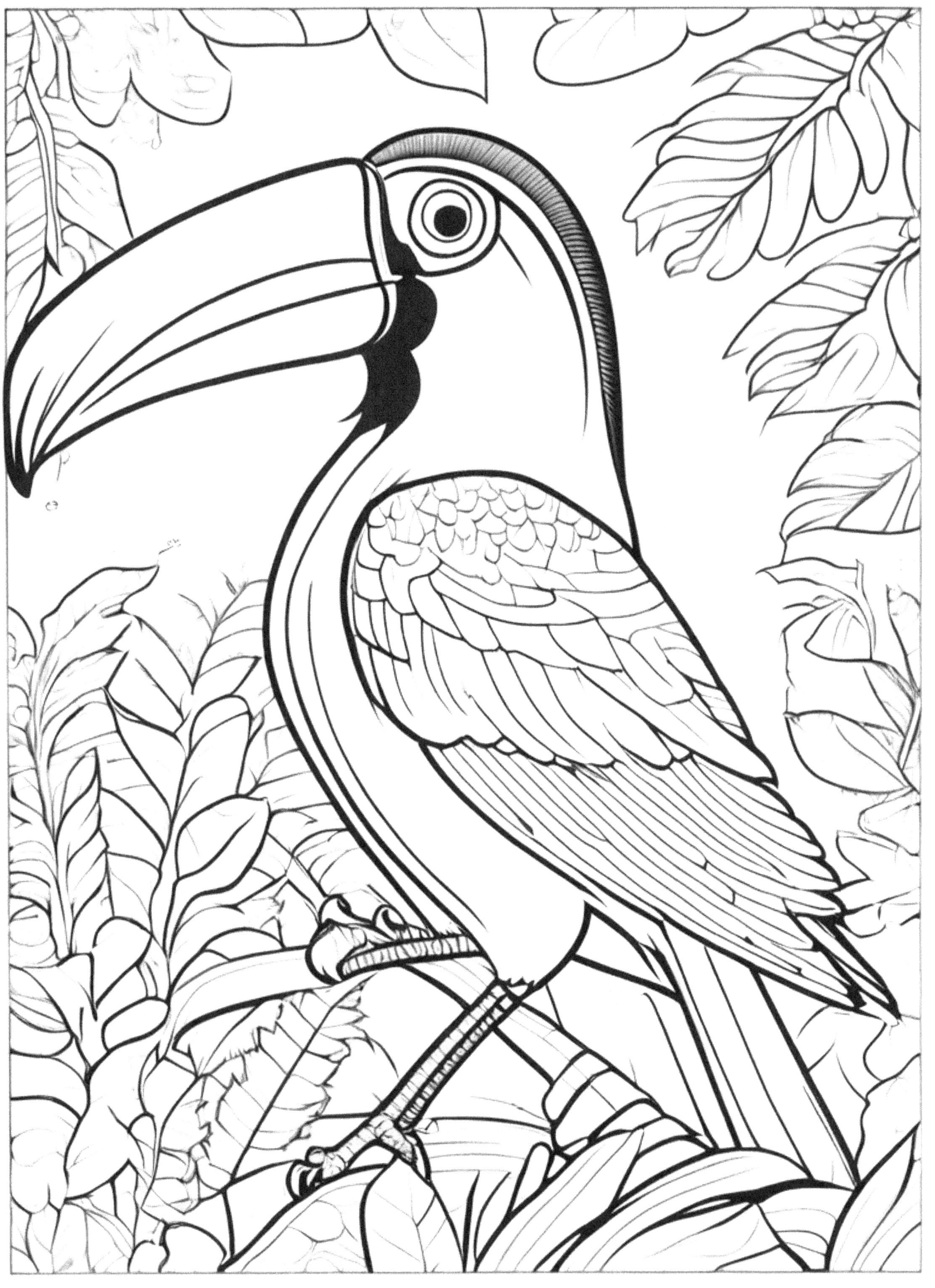

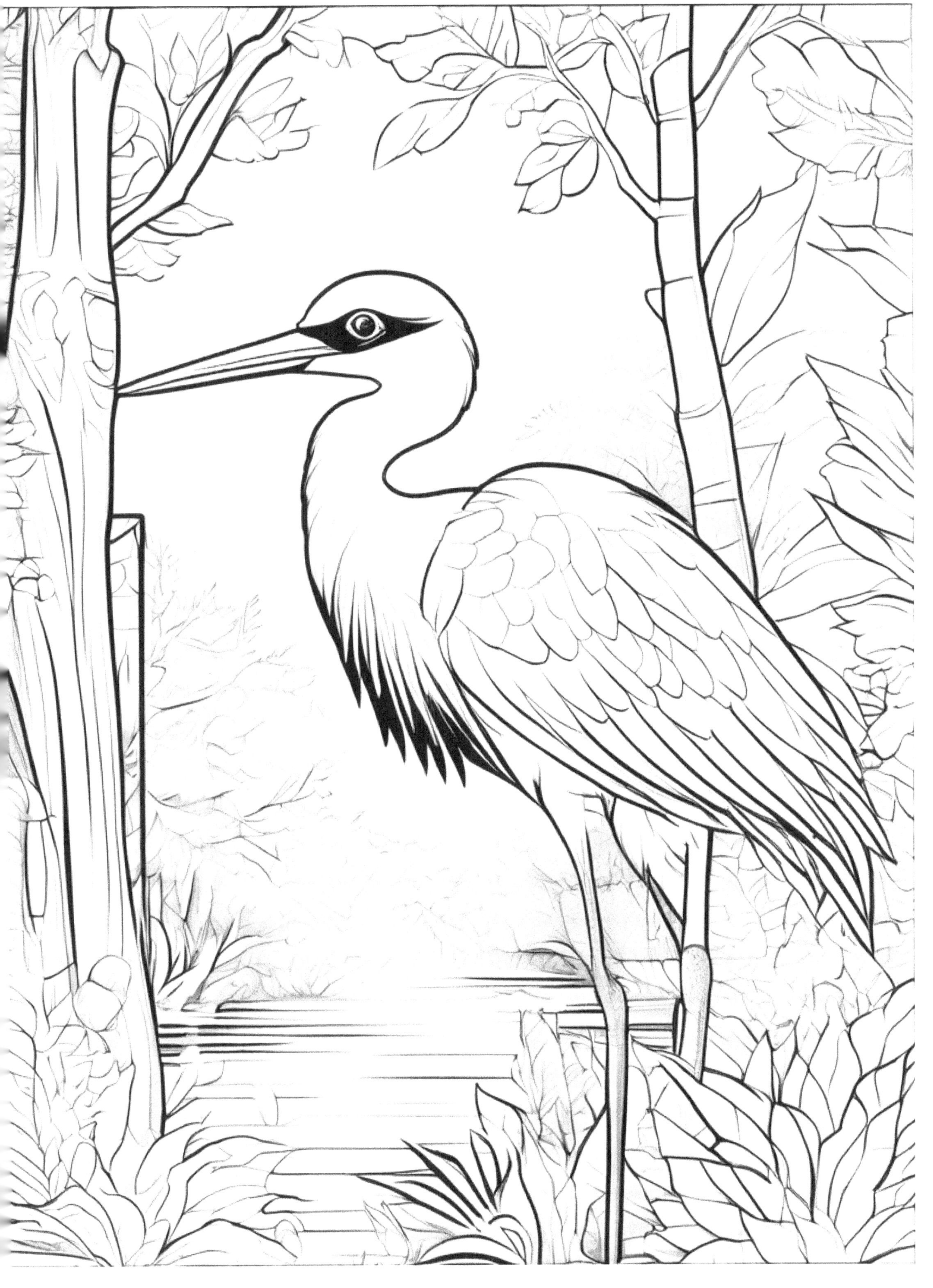

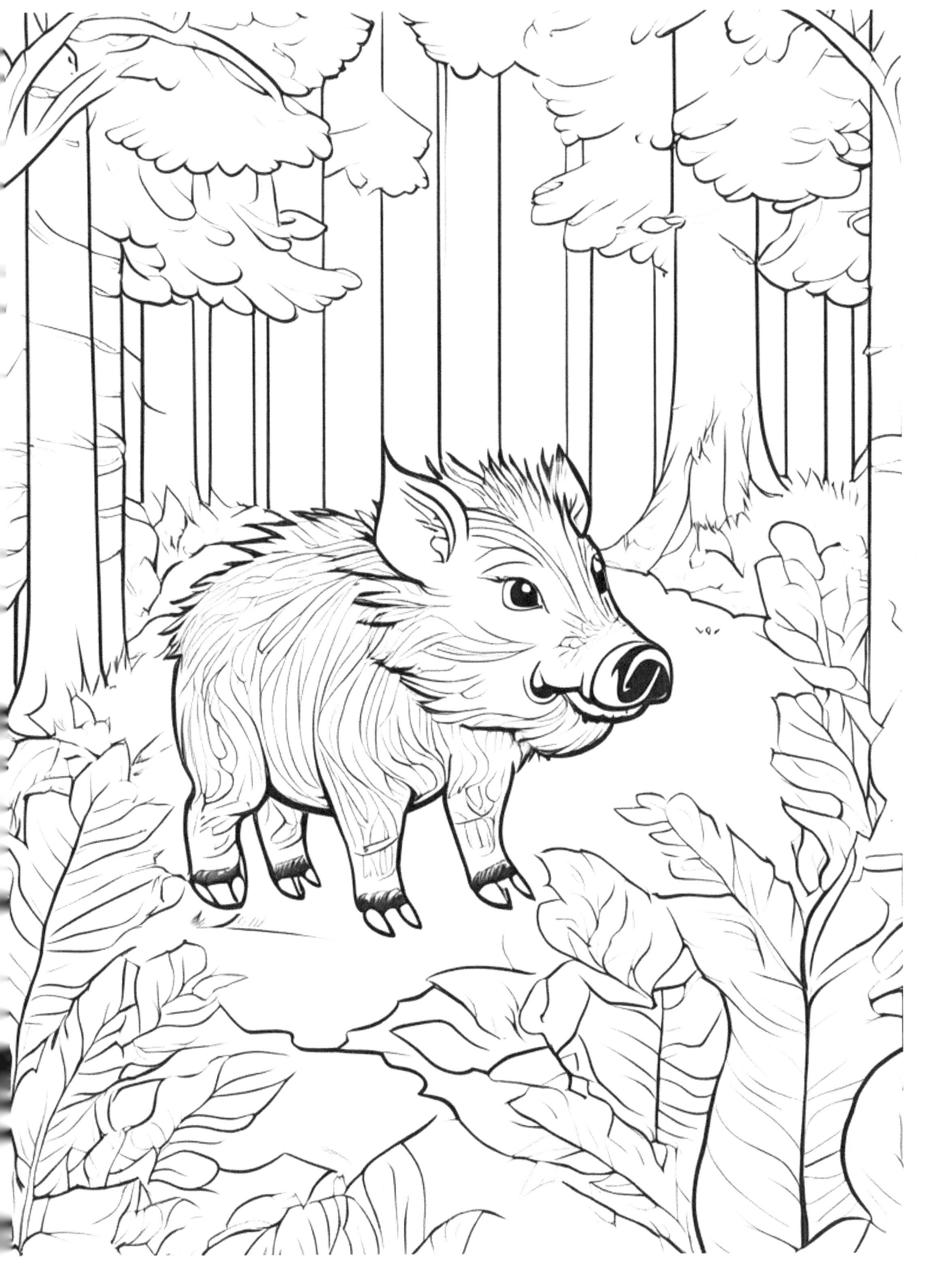

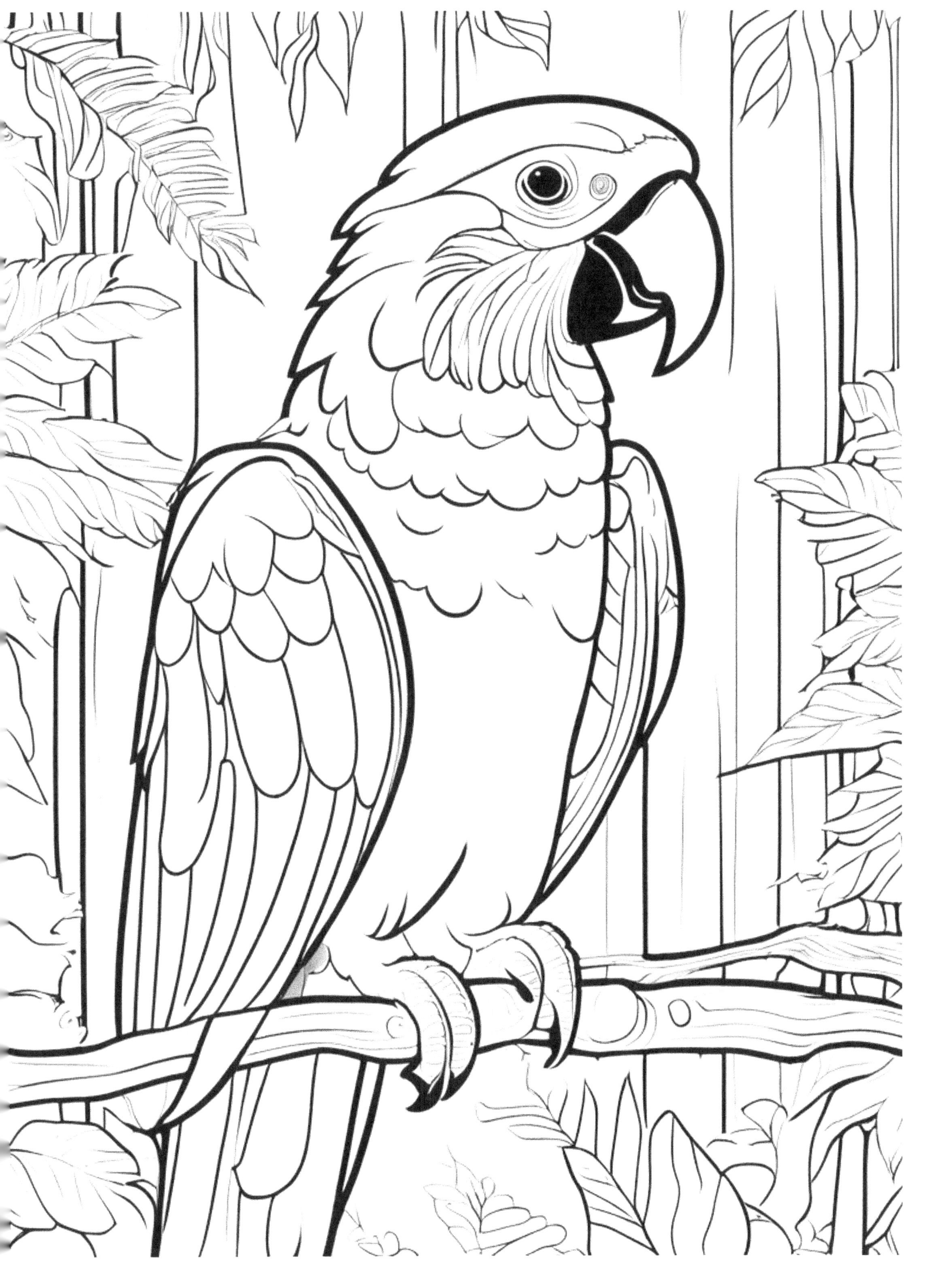

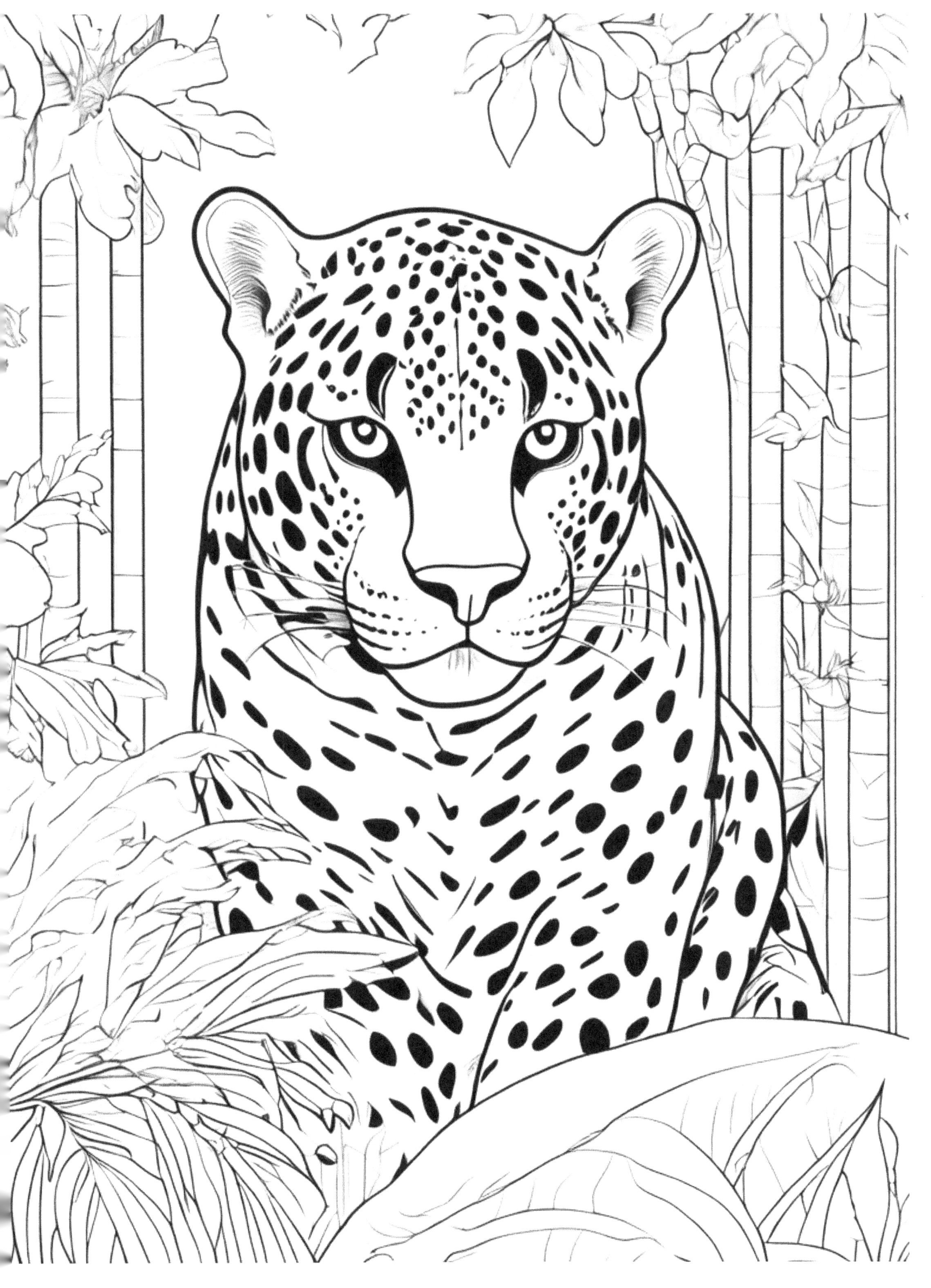

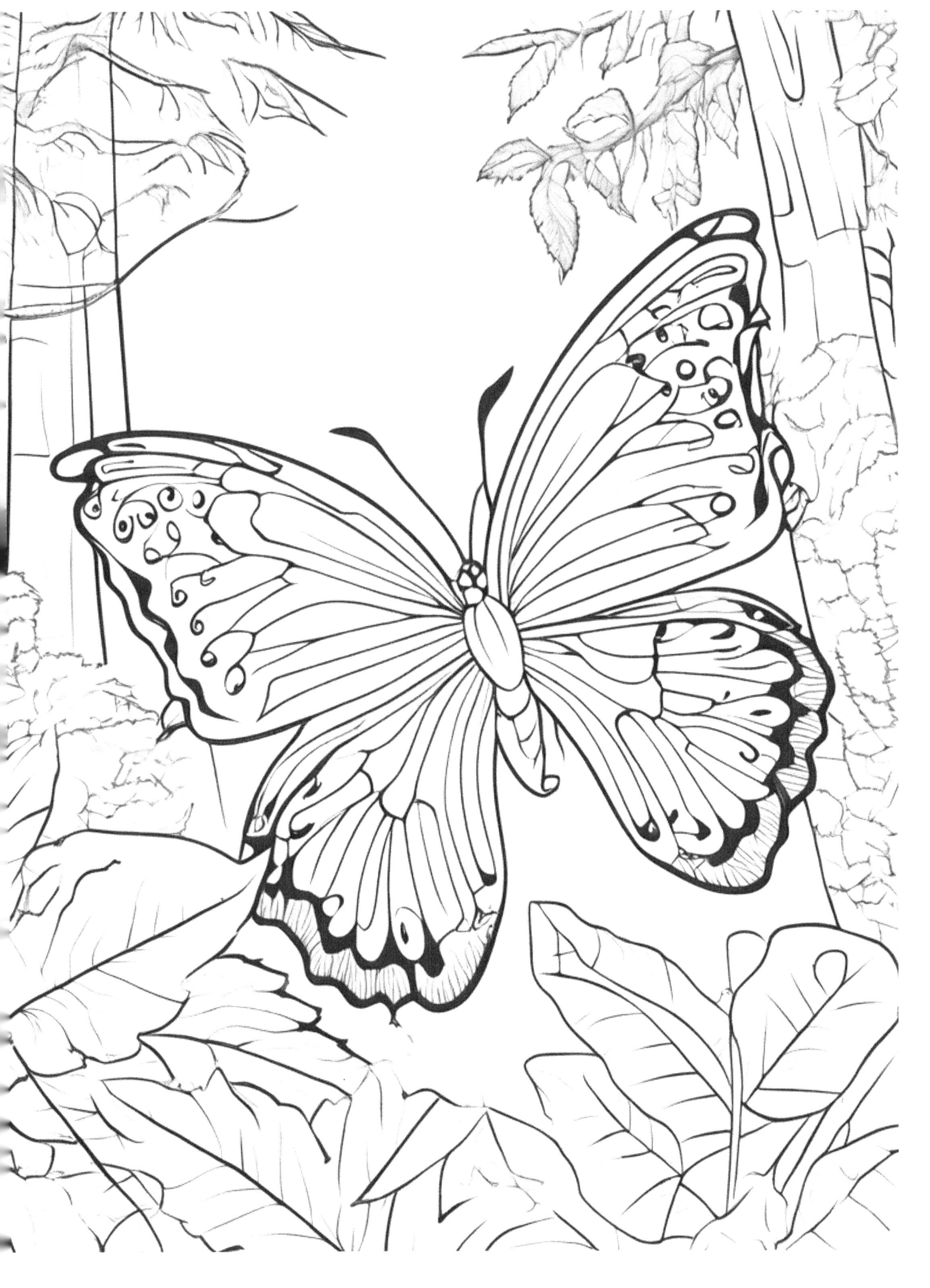

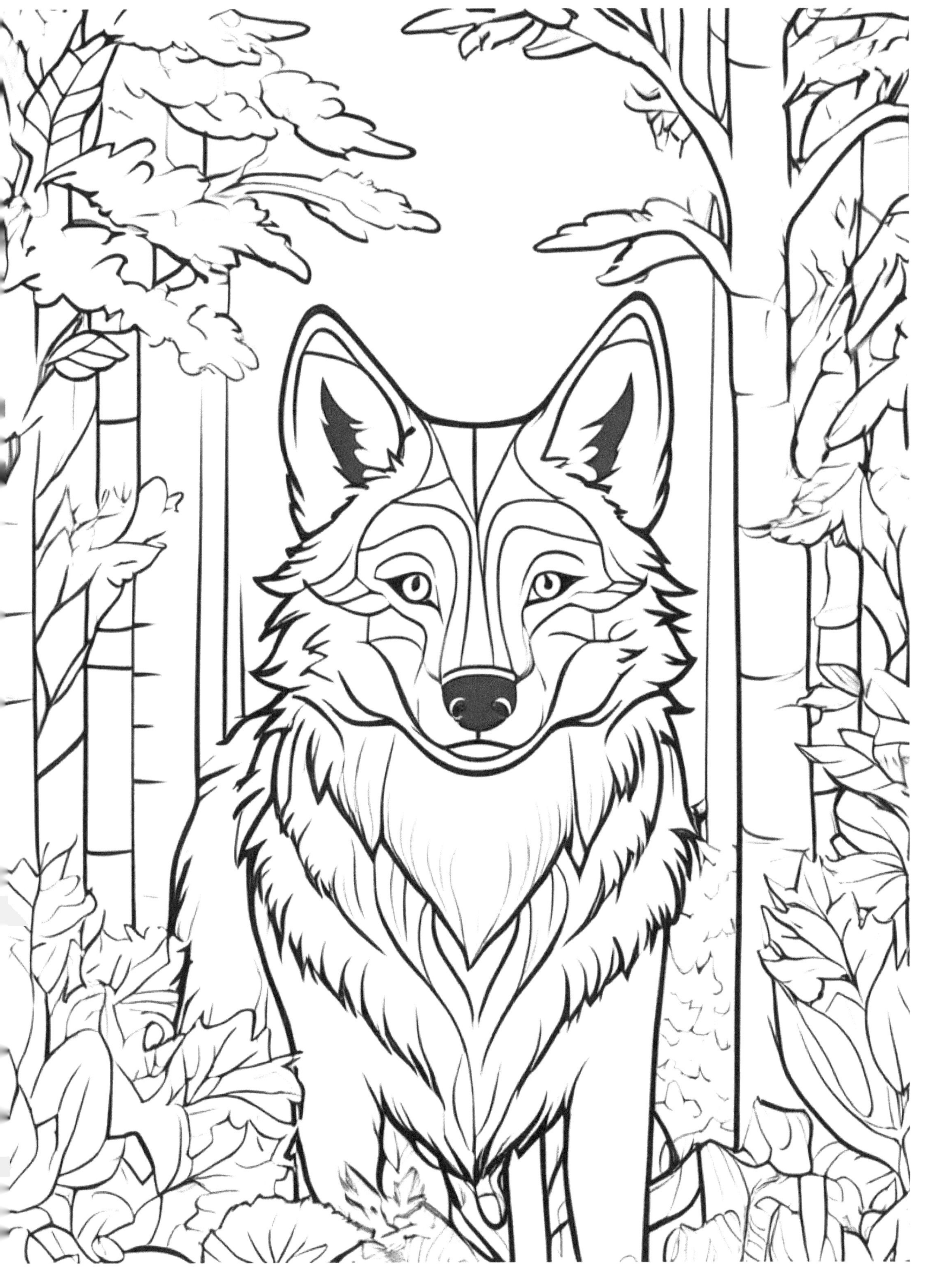

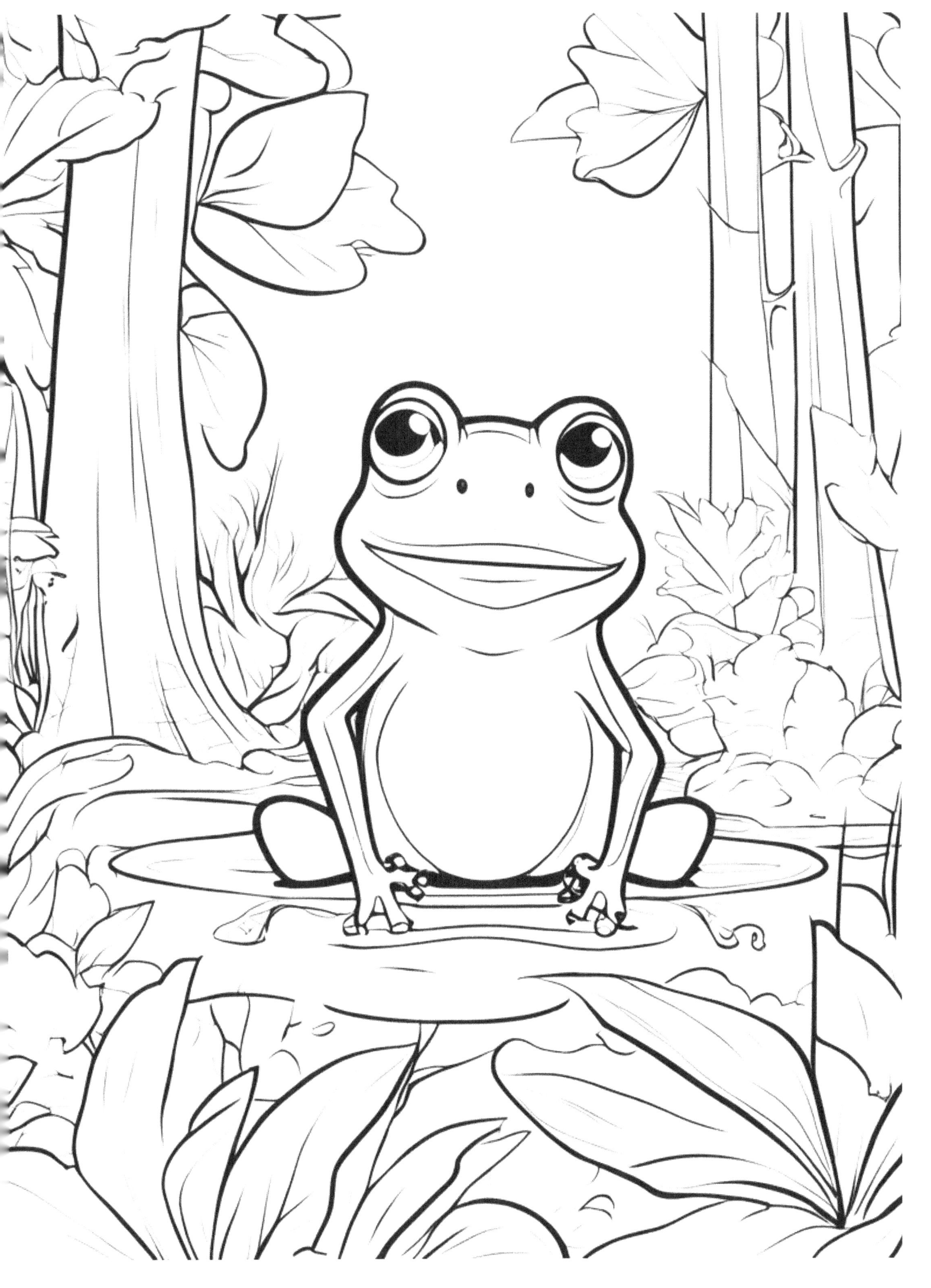

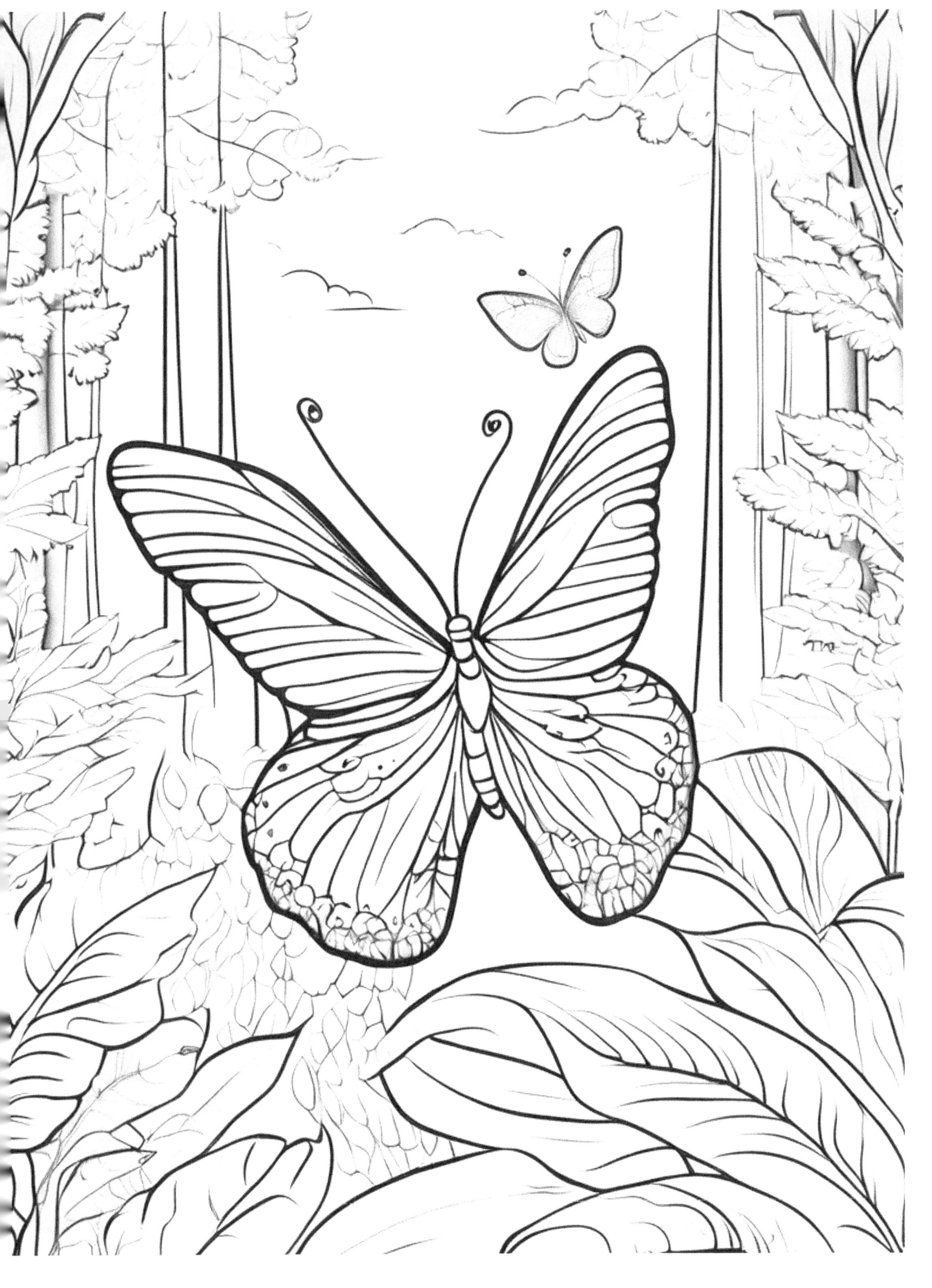

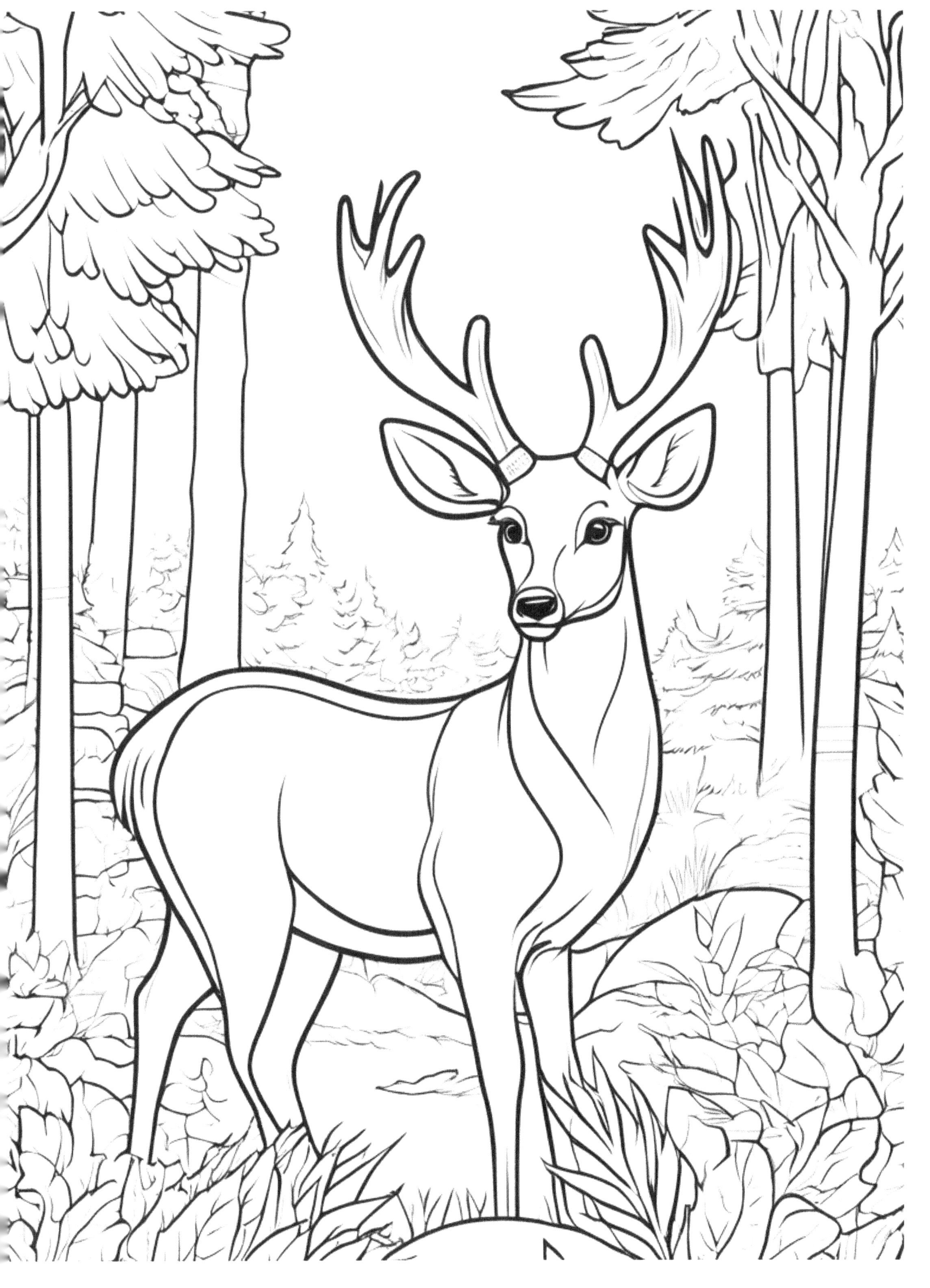

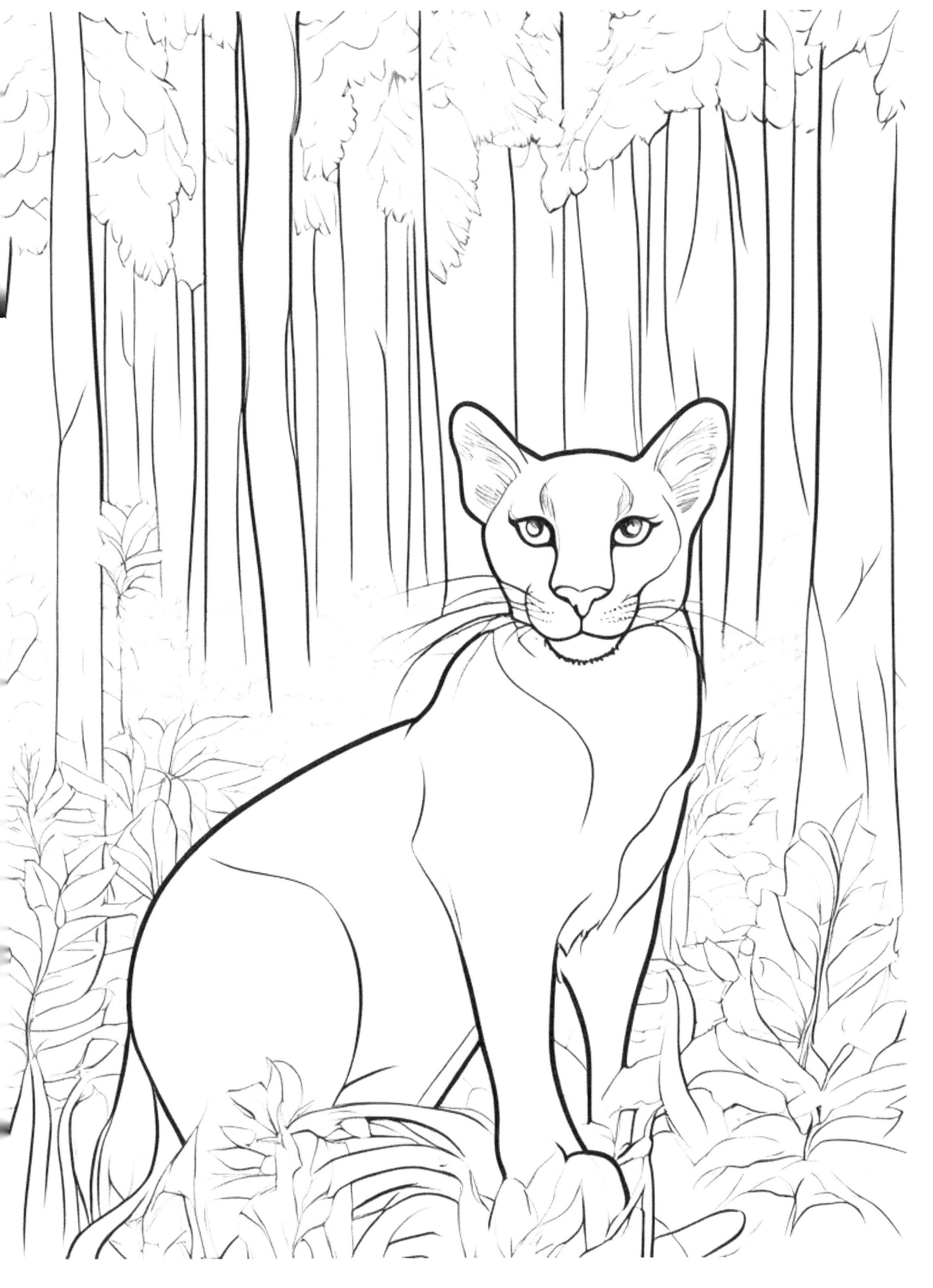

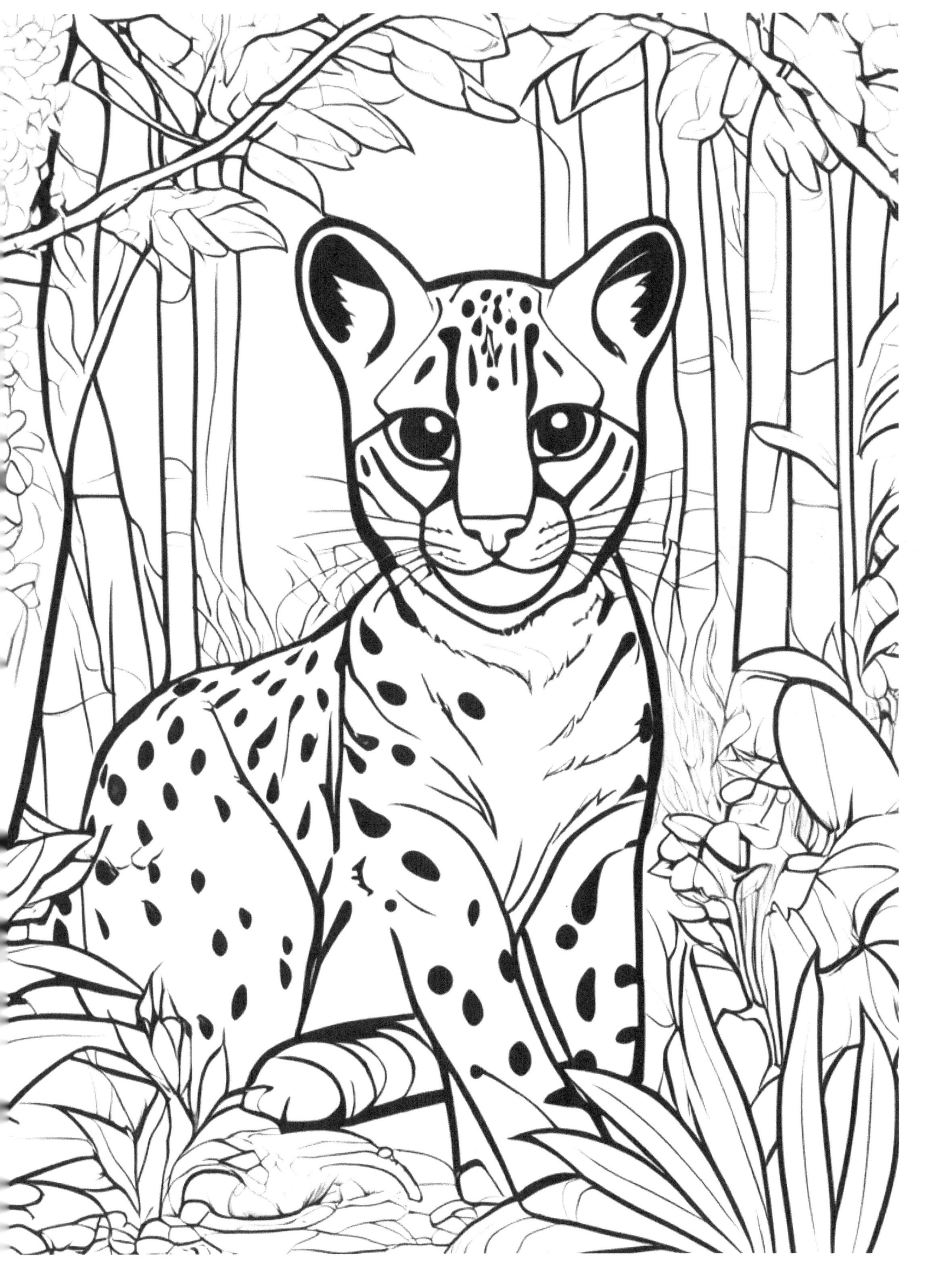

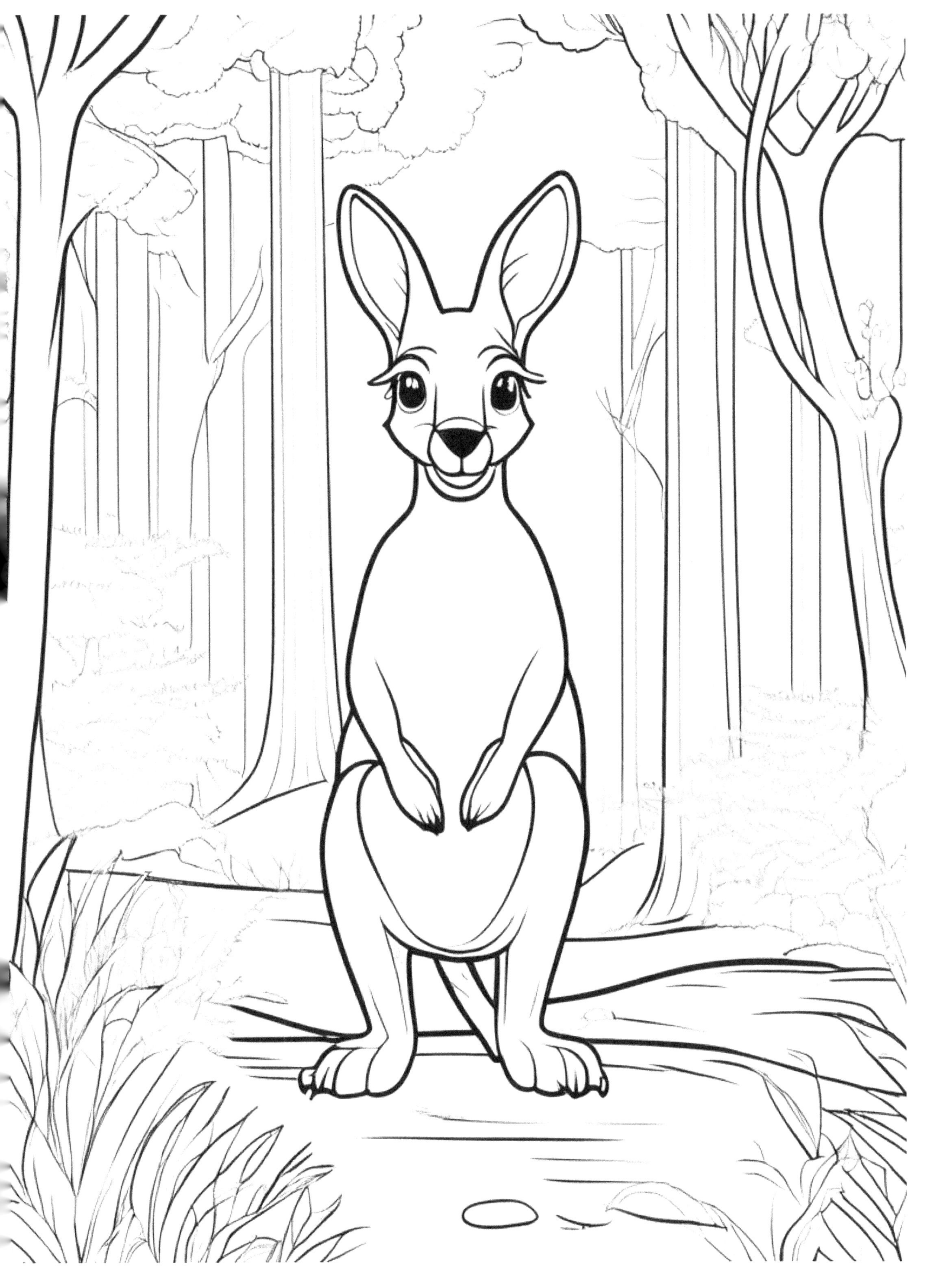

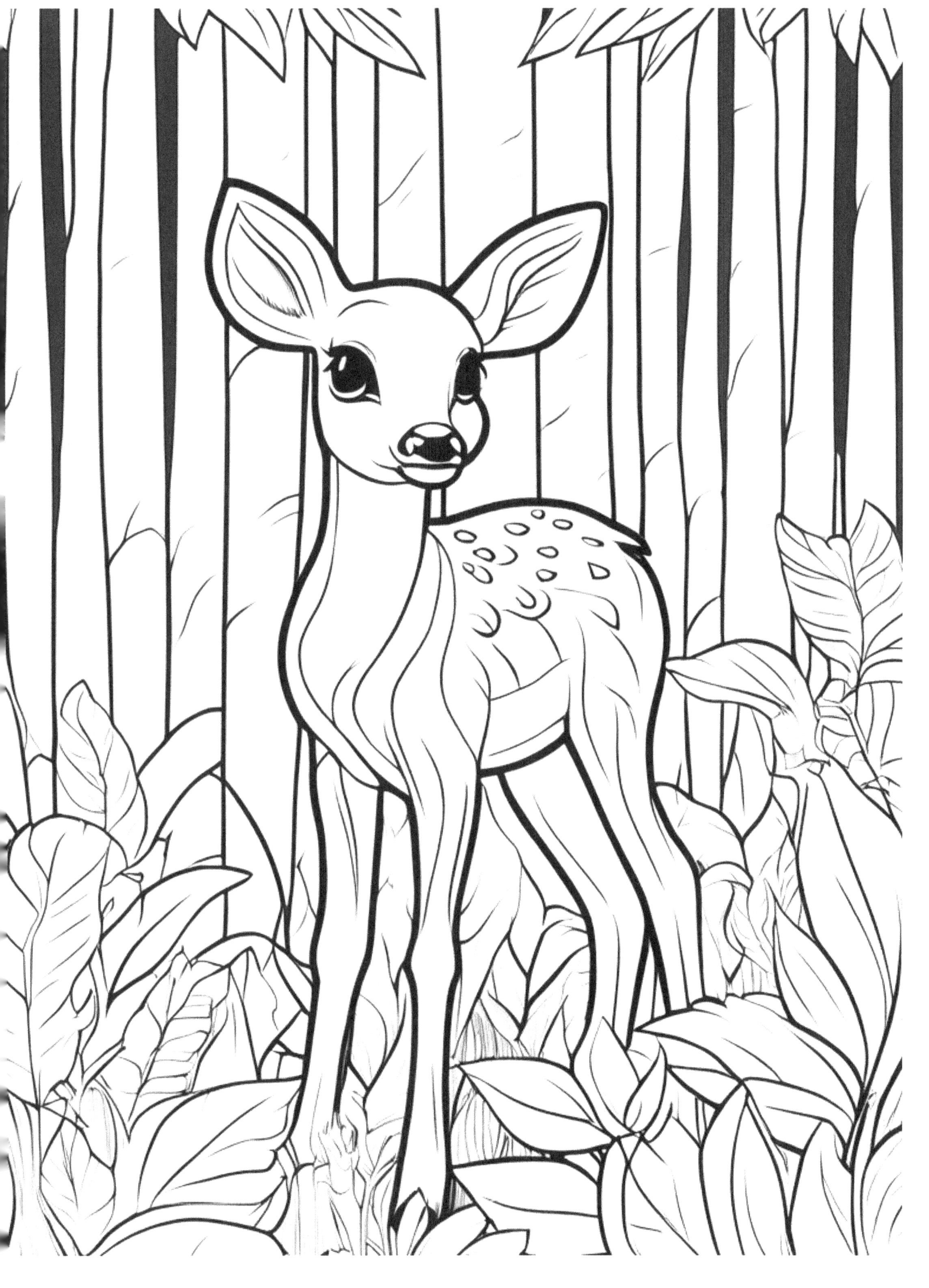

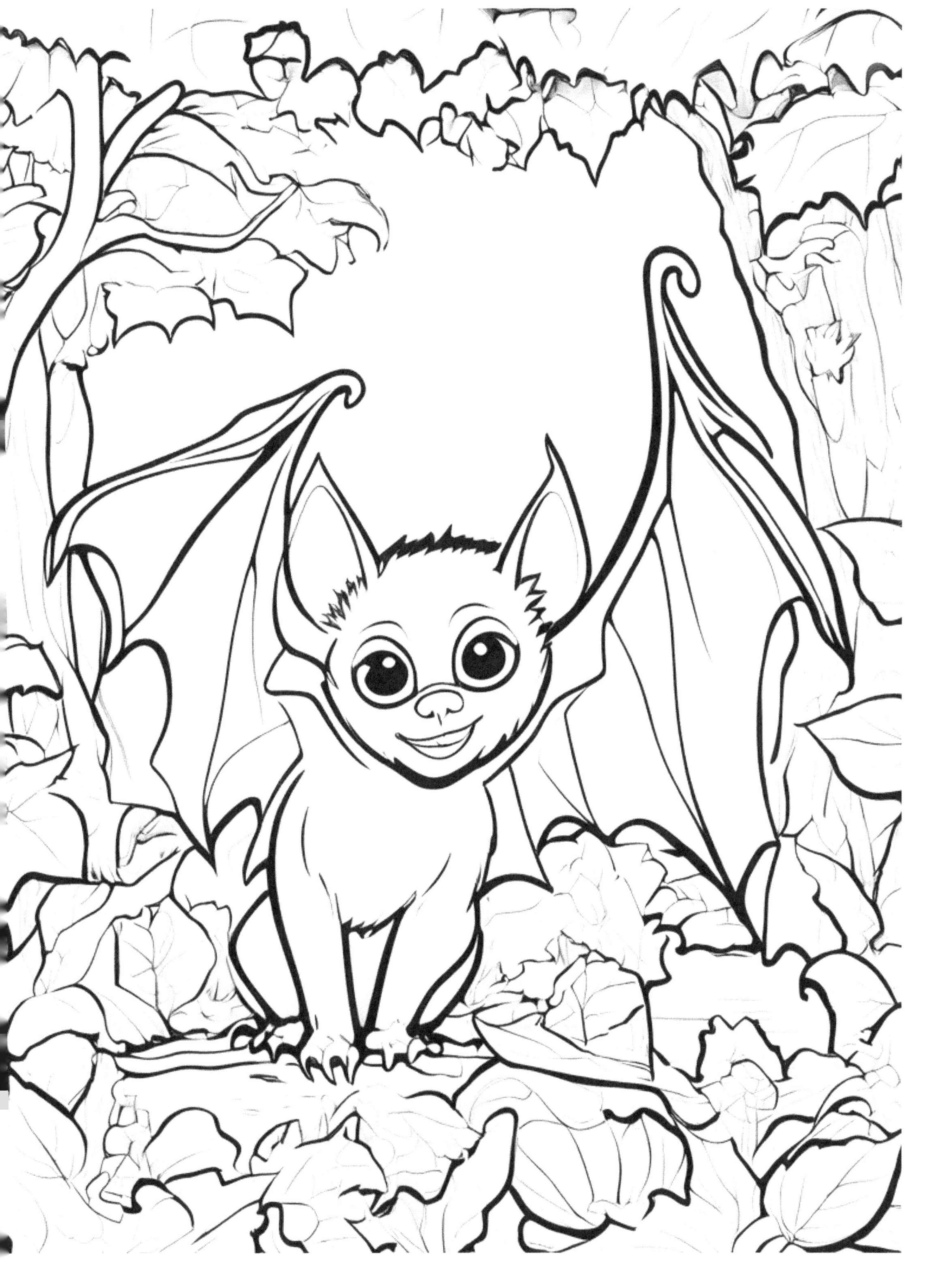

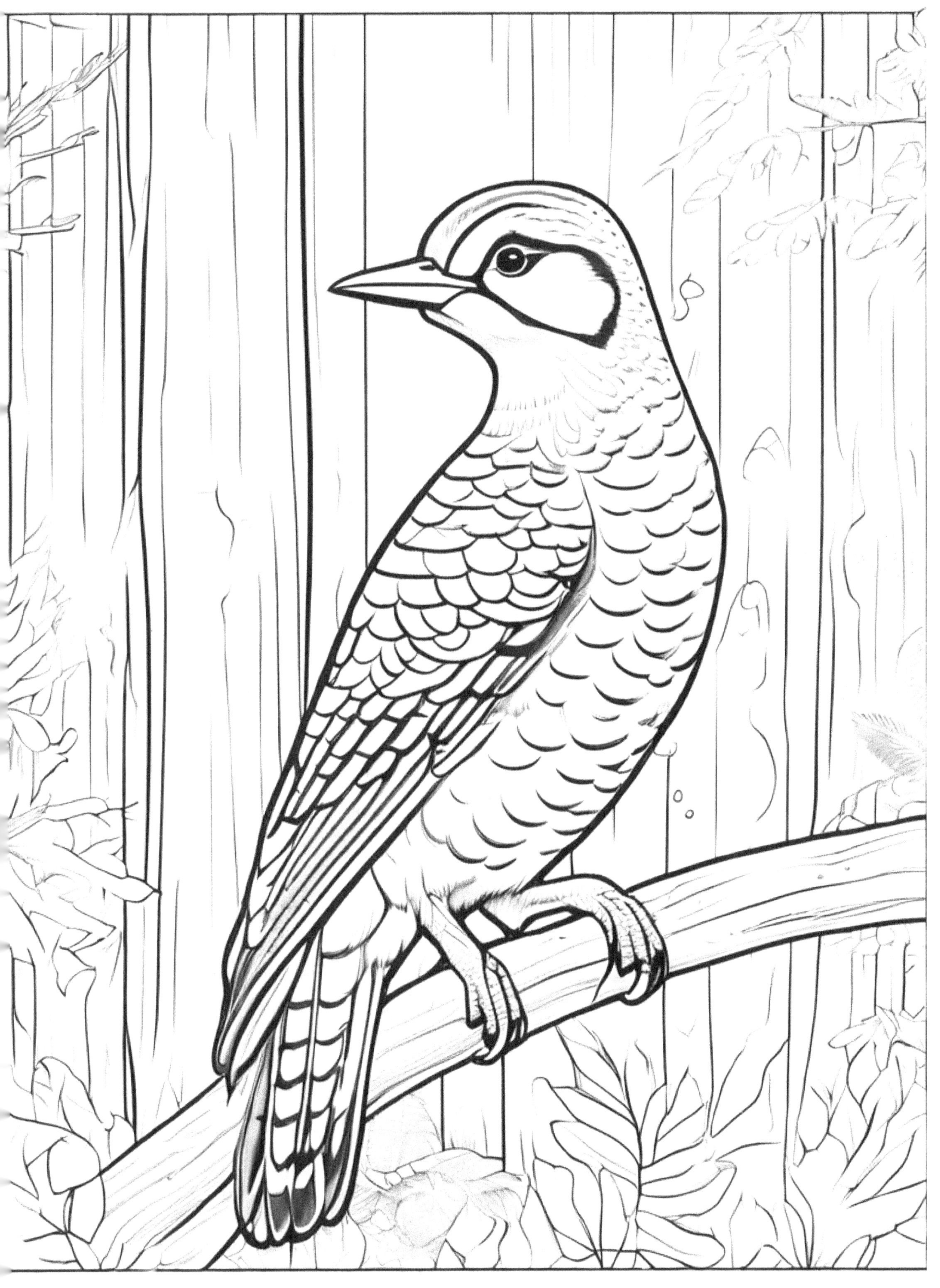

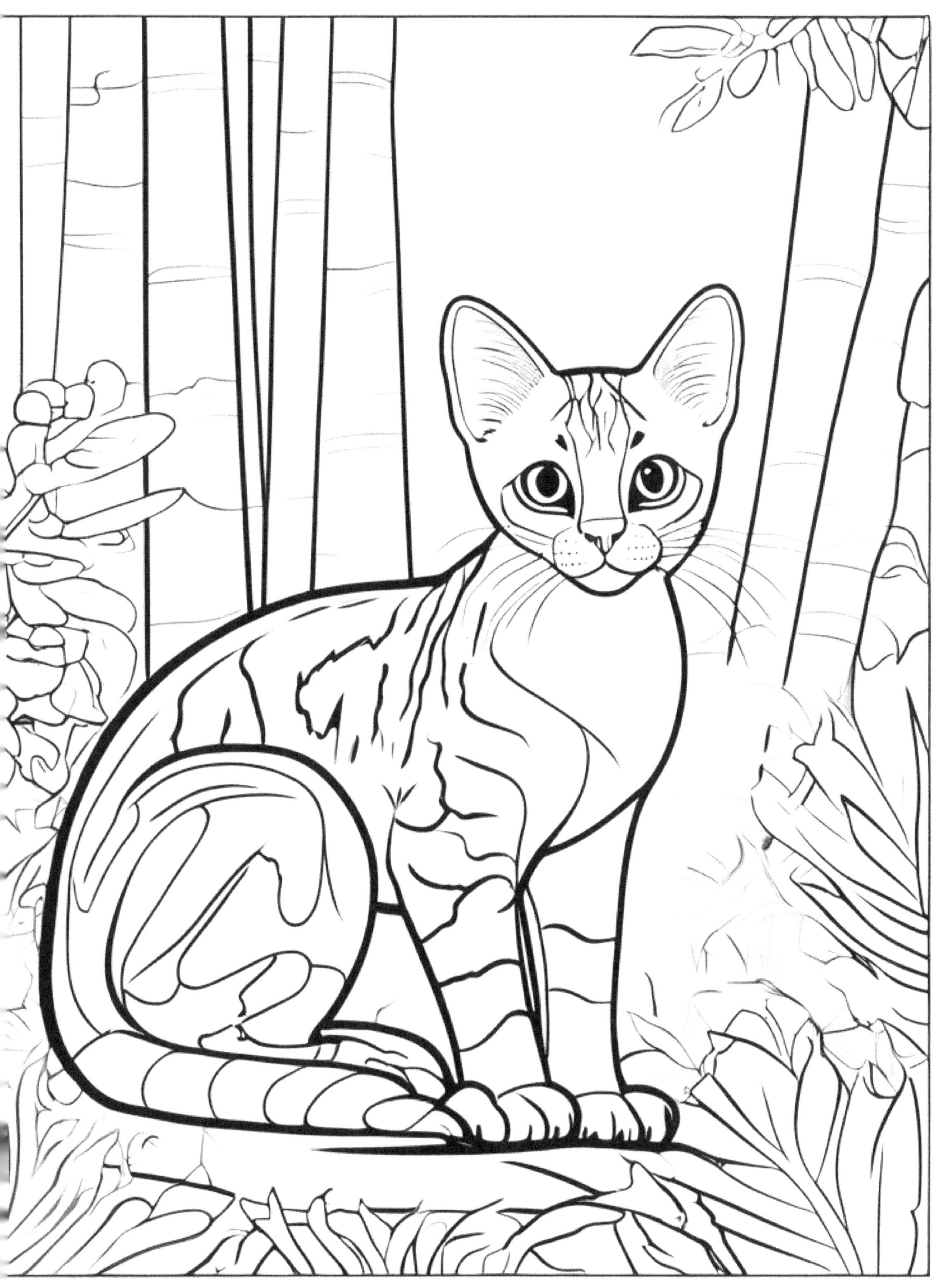

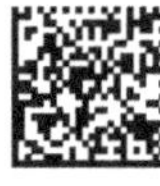
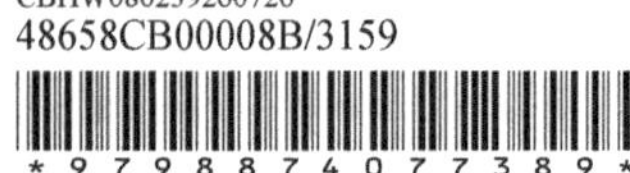